S0-BAN-929

HOMAGE TO RICHARD LINDNER

HOMAGE TO RICHARD LINDNER

Special issue of the XXe Siècle Review

Translations by: Joan Marie Weiss Davidson
© 1980 by Leon Amiel Publisher, New York
ISBN 0-8148-0724-0
PRINTED AND MANUFACTURED IN THE UNITED STATES OF AMERICA

Published by
LEON AMIEL PUBLISHER, INC.
31 West 46th Street
New York, New York 10036

Two lithographs by Richard Lindner

Richard and Denise Lindner
New York. 1968.
(Photo Richard Avedon.)

This special issue of XXe siècle on Richard Lindner, like the preceding issue on Wilfredo Lam, answers our need to grasp and comprehend one person and his work from different points of view. The solitary discourse of a writer on an artist sometimes has grandeur, but it inevitably gives rise to contradictions. The usual contributors to XXe siècle, Pierre Volboudt and Gilbert Lascault, are found here with Jean-Dominique Rey and Jean-Christophe Bailly, writing about the painter who, better than any other artist of his generation, has discovered the language of modernity of the second half of the twentieth century.

The specialists and friends of Richard Lindner, such as Werner Spies and Wolfgang Georg Fischer, have contributed their irreplaceable testimony and we have asked Maïten Bouisset to draw up the first chronology of this celebrated oeuvre which remains to a great extent unknown even to a well-informed and observant public. Thus we can pay homage to a German artist who began to make a name for himself in the United States at the end of the fifties, but who was anxious to divide his time between Paris and New York until the end of his life. The reputation of such a cosmopolitan painter could not be limited to his country of origin or to his adopted country. It is in the nature of certain painters to pass beyond all frontiers, rendering them ridiculous by the universality of artistic language. But it is Richard Lindner, the friend to whom we promised this work, the friend who hoped that the texts might be less numerous and more extensive than they generally are in our review, whom we wish to celebrate here. We miss his calm and his humor tremendously in these times of crises and perpetual questioning, and we would like to contribute to making them present here forever.

Alain Jouffroy

richard lindner
by werner spies

Themes:
1) Inequality of sexes - man is inferior

Frail, without the slightest sentimentality and quick with a caustic comeback, Richard Lindner created a pictorial universe in which he himself disappears as if into a cocoon. To him we owe those massive beasts, that sex injected with hormones, those mechanized beings and a world of psychological objects. In most of his paintings man and woman dramatize their unbearable otherness; only once, in the beginning, did Lindner replace the aggressive grimace à la Wedekind with an androgynous invention to which we shall return.

Central to the greatest number of his paintings, those at least of the last ten years, is New York, even after the urban folklore that marked them so strongly diminished. New York is more visible in the themes that study the effects of brutal shock and contrast than in those with a strictly American setting. This is the case in paintings such as *Solitary* and *The Ace of Spades*, both from 1973. One of Lindner's main themes, the inequality of the sexes, which in its uniqueness serves as a parable, is at the origin of the constant variations on the subject of the man facing the "Lindner-Venus" who is forced to emphasize his arrogant strength with padded shoulders and sharp, razor-blade creases in his trousers. Another symbol of masculine inferiority regularly appears in the motif of the card game in which the ace is always in the woman's hand.

Sex is so omnipresent in Lindner's paintings that it is considered the principal source of the artist's inspiration. Lindner, a painter of the libido? Certainly not Wesselmann fashion. With Lindner, sex represents the limit in relations among human beings, the impossible transgression of each individual existence. No doubt for this reason such introverted figures as Ludwig II and Proust assume a mythical function. In a complete withdrawal into himself, Lindner produces an androgynous fiction in which the power of evoking his own ego triumphs against all otherness in the real world.

In Lindner's work sex does not become, as it does in Warhol's, a product for consumption like Campbell's soup. It constitutes the most explicit symbol of the separation and the existential confinement of each person. From this perspective Lindner's work exhibits a depth and clarity of thought that surpasses pop art. In content his paintings are closer to the monomania of parables on life and the studio such as in Picasso's *The Painter and His Model*. Lindner's works conceal a peculiar ambiguity that is difficult to grasp and as tantalizing to Americans as to Europeans. Everyone in Lindner's work tries to pass off as other worldly exoticism what is merely a feeling of distance with respect to his own life.

Europeans view the simplifications (in Lindner's settings) as signals, the visual citations drawn from life in American cities. But there too there is a tendency to forget that the simplifications of the visual settings go back to Delaunay, Léger and Mondrian. Lindner comes off as the go-between who on each continent leaves a message that he himself understood. Therein lies the nerve center of the work, the element that gives it such efficacy. By renouncing spontaneity and identification, Lindner succeeds in creating a work that is deliberately somewhere in-between from every point of view.

During the last years of his life he spent a good portion of his time in his Paris studio. The emigrant shuttled back and forth between the old world and the new.

Earlier in his life, he would not have opted to do this. Too many painful memories were still attached to the city where, after fleeing Nazi Germany, he had spent some difficult years, years which were especially gloomy because of French chauvinistic attitudes. He felt the importance of the New York setting which was so exciting and which helped fashion him, the European exile, into a real painter.

New York, for Lindner, was never the city of the arts that it had become during the last decade of his life. The reason for changing scenes, however, cannot be entirely explained, especially since his life in Paris is hardly detectable in the paintings created at Place Furstenberg or rue des Saint Pères. Lindner remained a painter in exile, an exile that he asserted and carefully maintained. Perhaps his work necessitated the departure for Paris, requiring the artist's distance from the environment which he was in the process of painting. Such is the case with *East 69th Street*.

Lindner's behavior was by itself enough to separate him from the ideology of the here and now that pop art endlessly expresses. Consequently, he was not integrated socially or biographically into the American scene and very little connects his works to those of other American painters. Nor does he succeed in a natural way in introducing into his work the elements of daily life of a given country; he is lacking a naiveté that contact with the micro-myths as well as the social components of a neo-Dadaist renaissance would have given him. But he was too much of a skeptic anyway. He used the American environment consciously, submitted to its fascination, but never gave up his background, his European otherness. It was as if he gave himself up to some kind of ethnological research; and he integrated everything into his paintings which were still strongly influenced by his European memories.

We find ourselves faced with a rather unique case: a man in his fifties begins to paint, and at the end of twenty years, achieves a world-wide reputation. Before 1950, or even prior to that,

5

The Corset. *1954. Watercolor.*
74 x 59 cm. Private collection.

6

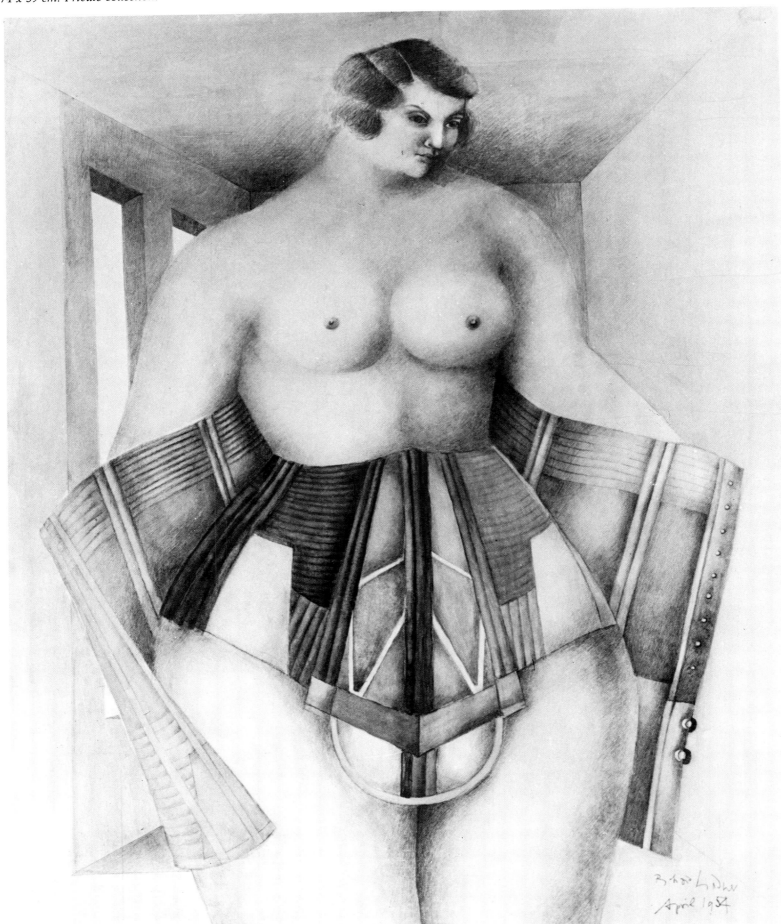

Portraits of Louis II of Bavaria which Richard Lindner used for his painting: **Ludwig II.**

nothing merits mentioning. Lindner was an illustrator, a popular designer and clearly a man who wanted to stick to his profession. Moreover, he never tried to give himself another image. The proof of this is in the remark made by his first wife who, upon learning that he had begun to paint, asked with an air of incredulity whether he was really capable of it. Lindner's work which raises the question of Lindner before Lindner — a simple question that is a contribution to the exegesis of the avant garde — leads us almost exclusively into the domain of actual experience, into the way of life and antipathies of the artist.

From whatever angle Lindner is examined, we always affirm the importance of his memories, memories which were preserved with such intensity since at the time Lindner began to recreate the events of an earlier time there had been no worthy interpretation of them. The actual experiences were not transformed into painting in stages so that all his lived experiences never seem directly related to a painting. A memory that is fifty years old manifests only when it becomes distant, a stranger to itself. Lindner begins to paint like someone who is not a writer begins to write his memoirs.

America had the effect of a catalyst. A world, that after the war began to believe in transcendental certainties and developed a constant in dealing with races and nationalities, found its esthetic symbol in the spontaneity of action painting. Reading the declarations of the painters and various spokesmen erases any doubt on this subject. As if it were programmed, the drift of postwar American esthetics, contrary to what was happening in Europe which was rooted in its history, was towards a process of tabula rasa. This produced a certain specific success for an artistic politics that was seeking its own independent beginnings; the influence of European immigration during the war had to be minimized.

The "universal style" of that era was based on a conscious rejection of the historical, of museum works. In a certain sense this rejection conditioned pop art, which, in choosing the American way of life and American consumption as its background, replaced the universal style with fabricated aspects of American life. Artists agreed in this choice of consumption, and considered it a way of defining a new kind of humanism.

Instead of confronting this optimism with irony, Lindner used this opportunity to associate his own origins and all that linked him to this commercial world with his new environment. The exile found what he needed to minimize the rupture that had occurred in his life. Against this backdrop he released his memories, which, as his first paintings show, borrow from American spontaneity the inclination for syncretic creation.

7

Lindner was interested in man, uniquely in fact in the man of the city. His creatures are swollen, fat and lavish to extremes. With women, everything is exaggerated in the right place; men show their neck and backs exactly as they have been depicted in the films of Eric von Stroheim. Rubber being without the slightest wrinkle, with hardly any faces, their expression comes from the martial-looking accessories they wear. Faces with sunglasses and eyes exaggerated in an ornamental way, fetishistic, resemble castings of the heads of gods. For the man, a hard and sharp profile; for the woman, a composition of bust, stomach, sex organ, all massively depicted. The latter is the golden calf of the libido Broadway style which becomes clearly fixed in the mind as one contemplates the showcases of the indescribable sex shops of 42nd Street. It is there that one finds all the insolence of city life — the Adam and Eve of a civilization in which accessories show the capacity for erotic greed.

Lindner's universe is one of disguise, one of the mask — a display intensified by clothing and objects; never do we encounter a nude body. The body forcibly complies with a rigorous grammar: corsets, laces, garters, suspenders, all kinds of undergarments spell out the underlying nudity. The fetishistic furor to which these heavy and powerful bodies are subjected has Sade as its model, and closer to our era, the cult dedicated to hooligans. It also has its formal models; the bold black lines crossing Fernand Léger's massive bodies greatly influenced Lindner who said: "For me Léger was most important. He was the only one to influence me. His life style inspired me and he was interested in everyday life. He was a peasant who charmed me. Elements of his paintings, the tools — all of it interested me." In fact, it would be an error to interpret the correlation between the body and the fetishes such as we find in Lindner in a purely psychoanalytic sense, that is, as a sign of sadistic submission. There is another equally important aspect: the collage bringing together body and objects. These two characteristics produce a dialectical game — the objects accompanying the body also constitute plastic phenomena by their very form and even before reaching the level of thematic correlations.

It is enough to make a tour of Lindner's New York studio where innumerable objects, scraps of reality, are carefully stowed away waiting to find their place in a composition. It is here that Lindner's European origins are most clearly revealed: the painting uses reality for its formal qualities and not just for its effects. The debate that went on between the Dadaists and the Surrealists cannot be ignored. One of Lindner's first paintings, The Meeting (1953), is a striking example of this. To analyze a work so carefully composed and meaningful — the only group portrait realized by Lindner — it is necessary to point out the pictorial citations and elements borrowed from Van Dongen, Hirshfield and Max Ernst. The woman who in the foreground turns her back to the viewer without doubt echoes Max Ernst's Weib, Greis und Blume (Woman, Old Man and Flower) of 1923-24, now

hanging in New York's Museum of Modern Art. Moreover, the upper part of the tightly-laced corset brings to mind the necklace in the form of a fan on the head of the woman in the Ernst painting. Looking closely, the upper part of the corset ends in a kind of cat's head. The head that the graphics of the laces delineate is at the same level as that of the tiger who is fixing his gaze on the viewer. This enigmatic encounter suddenly becomes clear: Lindner uses a system of references that we might define metonymically by a concept borrowed from rhetoric: the corset becomes a rhetorical figure corresponding to the animal of prey. What at first glance seems like a vague allusion is revealed to be a skillful game of mirrors: woman, the reflection of the animal of prey. Lindner gives us a double reading.

At first sight The Meeting resembles an exaggerated counterpart of American tourism with its display of memories, all of them equally weighted. It is clear, however, from the isolation of all the figures in the painting including those that really go together and by the different types that are grouped as in a theatrical photograph, that this painting is a departure point for future works. A transformation gradually touches the memory, its dependence on European literary models (Wedekind, Strindberg, Brecht) as well as artistic models (cubism, Duchamp, the new objectivity, Léger). In these paintings history is set down in the memory as if it were being recited by heart.

The props for the characters vary. Here Lindner's style is most clearly manifested. It amounts to a history of morals; everything here is opposed to nature and what is natural; there is no landscape, no nude and even the dogs are trained to assume a pose. The swollen flesh blows up the disguises and fetishes. Here reigns an unwrinkled immortality, an immortality of cosmetics.

The characters and their attributes are completely codified. The environment — Times Square and Coney Island — has been absorbed: the bodies and their environment blend to form a sort of brightly-colored and continuous epidermis. Lindner had to make a lot of sacrifices to succeed in this. It is obvious that he faced numerous problems. He stepped in everywhere that the environment furnished him with specimens permitting the structuring of the bodies. To the surrealist correlation between the object and psychology, to the disturbing, provocative atmosphere of the interiors by Balthus that Lindner studied, to the encounter between monstrously precocious children playing with hoops and well-dressed visitors, are added Lindner's attempts to give a new expression to certain figures through the processes of enlargement and distortion.

Lindner's method is to break up the female form much as the cubists did. The body is decomposed into its functioning parts and then assembled into an erotic puzzle. The body takes on a new significance. This is instrumental for the cubist's freedom and recalls the first cubist efforts establishing the famous analogies between the body and musical instruments. In another series of works — among them Stranger

Stranger No. 1. *1958. Oil on canvas.*
127 x 70 cm. Mr. and Mrs. Herman
Elkon collection, New York.

Stranger No. 2. *Oil on canvas.*
152.5 x 101.5 cm. The Trustees
of the Tate Gallery, London.
(Photo Cordier and Ekstrom.)

9

II (1958) — Lindner borrows certain formal methods from Chirico; in *One Afternoon* (also 1958) he gave up an architectural construction and used fragments of shapes that the viewer who is initiated into the pictorial language of the cubists can assemble into a continuous picture and relate to complementary methods of gestalt psychology. The initial paintings vary. The influence of Duchamp is also perceptible — not only the negative aspects of Duchamp which gave rise to some of Lindner's anticultural reactions — but also Duchamp, the cubist.

In the works *Telephone* (1966) and *Ice* (1966) the poster quality is apparent. Lindner used the shapes and effects of color from the techniques of the American school and adopted them to his own figurative obsessions. By reducing all the problems of painting to the human figure, the painting is brought to the point of expressing only itself. The acceptance of reality, the admira-

tion of the vital American spirit which denies old age and brutality in a manner that borders on the unsophisticated — all this is found in his figures, charged with the real trappings of civilization, the heraldic symbols of urban society.

Only in our first impressions do we feel a certain strangeness and the extent to which this sensitive European, tossed from one country to another, recklessly shocked the American school of painting; in the glistening pop-style landscape, transposing all the elements to the proportions of a new world, Lindner registered his protest against the society of the twenties. The machine-man, lacquered in hues of ice cream, no longer runs dangerous risks; he works or he doesn't, like the flippers on the pinball machines of the penny arcades along Broadway lit streets.

Particular attention should be paid to Lindner's drawings and preliminary sketches. Widely-spaced lines divide the characters and the objects and test the effects produced on the canvas by contrasting colors. At this stage Lindner's response to a new idea or borrowed motif is also apparent. Then, very quickly, the discovery he made in the real world is metamorphosed into his signature and is inserted in his inventory of already existing forms.

Between the sketches and the completed painting, Lindner produced gouaches and colored pencil drawings on a large format. In these he achieved a perfection that excites even those viewers who are tempted initially to give up before certain canvases. Lindner offers a visual pleasure reminiscent of the drawings of Juan Gris or Léger. The eye follows everything that deviates from the natural order and from what seems possible and it does so with such docility that it does not see the disproportion between the content and the magic of its representation.

It is here too, that Lindner, moved by a true craftsman's passion, began to oppose mass production and the process of reproduction. His fascination with everything that conformed to a norm, whatever importance he attached to that norm, is scarcely reflected in his style. Maintaining his position as an intermediary, he surveyed the asphalt American landscape trying to discover those elements that would suit his personal interests. The world of Bavarian toys, Bavarian Baroque and literary and political myths are projected into an environment that stood for immediate gratification, the best return on a commodity, a body or an idea.

Despite his fascination with the inventions of a world that lives only for the present, Lindner's message should be placed in the domain of anesthesia and the dance macabre.

Lindner owes his fame to pop art. His works reveal a number of its elements, but the roots go back to other areas: back to an intellectual work which shares a nostalgia for the present; the fascination of young Americans for consumption, and the clichés of their civilization. But since spontaneity awakens a certain suspicion Lindner is lead towards a contrary interpretation although his message was scarcely noticed amidst the banal, imprecise style of that era. It is tempting to see Lindner differently and to acknowledge him as the most original representative of the synthesis between European and American creation. The unique character of Lindner's work should be considered against this background.

During the last ten years of his life Lindner took up living in Paris again. To speak of his return to Europe, however, would be an exaggeration. Lindner himself rejected this view and felt it suited art politicians who liked to contrast the two art centers. He settled down in France to relive an important contradiction: his relation to the past that the American taste for reality and novelty constantly stifled. "I juggle with the past," said Lindner. "I paint post cards representing the rural summer holidays of my past." What fascinates Americans contemplating his work — "Lindner's love of the secret" — tells us Europeans quite another story, perhaps one that explains this American propensity to fabricate mythologies without recourse to the secretive with its roots in everyday life, and to confer an emotional charge that is so great that real time stops for a few moments and preserves the illusion of eternity. As culture, pop art was the best example of what we succeed in grasping and imitating with difficulty, that transformation of commodities into what could be termed cultural goods and cultural goods into what we are accustomed to defining as commodities. In my opinion, no other work reveals and exploits in such a critical manner the gap between the American and European scenes. And the apparent convergence that Lindner's work sparks only increases the difficulty of understanding the reciprocity between the two cultures. In two of his paintings the artist tries to correct the malaise that is aroused by the interpenetration of two universes unacquainted with each other. Let us point them out: the portrait of Proust executed in Europe in 1950 and the epitaph for Marilyn Monroe painted in the United States in 1967, *Marilyn Was Here*, the portrait and the last somewhat schematic love song to an idol; in the first, the thorough search for a man who based his work on his personal experience and in the second, the search for a Hollywood idol, forced by the system to expose her body to constant pictures which live on today, well beyond her death; an historical public institution, a pure product of American masculinity at the disposal of everyone; two images that Lindner offered from a kind of cold trance in which the work nearly produced itself. Today the portrait of Proust, hardly known in the past, seems more and more like a key work among Lindner's paintings. It continues to be the great fiction of beginnings that succeeded in spite of the fact that it opened the way to the voracious dialectic between man and woman. What precedes this painting scarcely matters. The *Portrait of Proust* closes the career of the illustrator, the designer and the Sunday painter. Lindner was nearly fifty years old at the time. He painted this portrait during a sojourn of several months that he made to Paris after the war. It is touching to see that the return to Europe in search of a world which had been his and which he found in ruins led him to the search for Proust. Naturally, the Proust painting ought to be counted heavily in an output that was limited to five to ten paintings a year. Why did Lindner choose Proust? He himself never knew. However, many writers were his friends and Lindner admits that he felt more

The Target No. 1. *1960. Oil on canvas. 152 x 102 cm. (Photo Cordier and Ekstrom, New York.)*

12

Woman in Corset. *1961.*
Oil on canvas. 102 x 51 cm.
Mme. Andre Bloc collection.

at ease in their presence than in the company of painters. Like the writers, Lindner had an inimitable gift for recapturing memories and seizing the moment in an aphoristic form. He was one of those rare artists, for example, to have good relations with Céline in whom he found a humanity that others who knew him never discovered. Lindner met Gide, Malraux, Brecht, the Mann brothers ("Heinrich was the more gifted of the two; the other one simply spoke better German"). Lindner said: "What fascinated me about Proust was his impudent egotism. Look at my painting. The portrait turns in on itself; it is concerned only with itself. I find something immodest in this portrait." Lindner recreates their encounter which allowed him to pin down his opposite and sketch the immortal quality that marked his subject. We are reminded of what impelled Sartre to write his *Flaubert*, that is, that Flaubert's world no longer existed; it was finished and could be comprehended only through documents. Like Sartre, Lindner manipulated dead things with a certain fascination; it seemed to provide him with a raison d'être for his own existence without any element of sentimentality. The need to analyze and dissect led both Lindner and Proust to autobiography. Lindner declared that he engaged in many hours of study before he undertook his *Proust*: "The most difficult thing for me was to forget Proust's real appearance since we do not paint people as they are; we paint the effect they produce."

This brings to mind Picasso's work on the portrait of Gertrude Stein. In the spring of 1906 she posed for Picasso more than sixty times. Ultimately Picasso exclaimed in a fury: "When I look at you, I no longer see you," whereupon he left Paris for several months and painted Stein's portrait upon his return without ever seeing her again.

Lindner questioned people who had known Proust, presented them with sketches and then compiled the advice he received; in particular, he noted the statements of a bookseller and Jean Cocteau. The result was that the icon intently closed in on itself. "Everyone with whom I spoke detested him. I didn't hear a single friendly word." And: "He was the kind to write only about himself and he lived only for himself. A Picasso type except that he had no weaknesses. Picasso isn't a mean person. He has nothing of the primitive or the instinctive; with him everything is intellect — a mortal weapon."

In comparing Lindner's *Proust* with the well-known portrait — that pretty, fashionable, trifling thing — by Jacques-Emile Blanche, or with the testimonies of friends and contemporaries, Lindner's work has an unmistakable psychological verity. Colette spoke of ceremonial garments. Léon-Paul Fargue found the portrait brought out "the complexion of a man who no longer breathes by day." Finally, Edmond Jaloux wrote: "He seemed to be emerging from a nightmare. He had decided never to give up the fashions of his youth — a very high stiff collar and starched shirt. One was facing both a child and a very old mandarin." The effect of the portrait is to upset us which brings us closer to the obsessions of Lindner himself and also to what, beyond the thematic, was to determine the artist's style from then on. The head seems to be stuffed into armor, a knot strangles the neck and gives the appearance of a corset as in the portrait of Marilyn; however, Proust's high collar seems to be sliding down. Half of the face is bluish. Here one thinks of the asthma attacks Proust suffered. Here is a head which seems cut off in the shelter of ramparts. A comparison can be made with two drawings, Picasso's *Apollinaire blessé* (Apollinaire wounded) and Max Ernst's *Portrait of André Breton*. Bandages have always aroused Lindner's interest; nowhere in his later work will we find a plain nude undecorated or unequipped with some sort of fetish.

In the process of searching for his Proustian model, Lindner brought his own memories to the conscious level. In fact, it may be asserted without exaggerating that all the portraits of future years would have been unthinkable without the *Proust*. Corsets, books with laces, riding breeches, whips, children whose plump and lymphatic bodies seem to choke in their Sunday clothes, in a universe tied up, strangled with sadism, reminiscent of the terra cottas by Andrea della Robbia or nursing infants in a Florentine hospital! Again, corsets, paddings remind us of the couturier's manikins, of flesh looking like sawdust, children swollen as if filled with air and surrounded by pointed machines and gigantic toys. For Lindner this lost world represents the replacement of products. But the painted toy also threatens children or may cause them to burst like a balloon. The world of toys from his Nuremberg childhood remained a fascinating euphemism, signifying the iron maiden, the pillory or games for executioners. ("Sade refined a literature that was not reality; the iron maiden existed.") Eventually, the *Proust* is shifted onto a theatrical plane. Lindner's fascination with androgynous beings has been mentioned before. This *Proust* with mustache and feminine curls, a prisoner of the collar, is one illustration of it — an interpretation which Lindner himself confirmed. "When I portray couples, the man is always the weaker. Proust is an exception. He is both male and female, the total portrait. An absolute."

Proust's portrait, it is revealing to note, was followed by several portraits of children in which the libido, apparently neutralized in the Proust, is excited upon contact with toys or some kind of variation of a purely mechanical game. These paintings are deeply sexual. Walter Benjamin, a collector of toys defined the

Rock-Rock. 1966-67. Oil on canvas. 178 x 152.5 cm. Dallas Museum of Fine Arts. (Photo Geoffrey Clements.)

14

Portrait of Marcel Proust. *1950*
Oil on canvas. 71 x 61 cm.
Max and Lynda Palevsky
collection, Los Angeles.

Preparatory sketch for
Marilyn was here. *1967.*
(Photo Piotr Trawinski.)

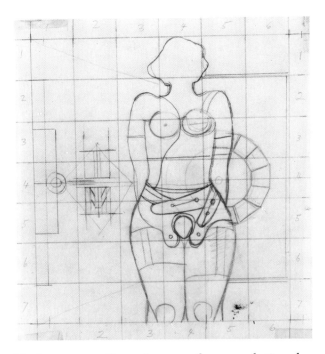

libidinous quality of toys, the correlation between toys and fetishism: "The alabaster bust of which the 17th century poet sang belonged only to dolls whose existence was fragile and risky." Lindner's studios were filled with all kinds of knicknacks from Nuremberg, a large number of which are found in his paintings. On the erotic level, they don't express much. Man and woman meet but scarcely make contact. Only the props and secondary figures feel and touch each other. This is an eroticism of machines that brings to mind Duchamp, and the contrasts between the forms of Léger which in the thirties implied more than a simple meeting of objects. Man and woman are surrounded by a well-oiled cosmos. The brilliant lacquers that have been progressively added on to the canvas furnish an exciting makeup. The intensity of this dividing up of bodies into parts far surpasses the one-dimensional irony of the pop artists (with the exception of Warhol who attains mythic dimensions), and shows the extent to which Lindner's work is stamped by the European context. Freud, Wedekind, Strindberg, Stuck and Klimt did not merely exercise an influence that escaped Lindner during his research on Proust. They form a conscious prolongation of myth. What Lindner tells us about relations between the sexes, about their inequality which in his paintings is always expressed at the man's expense, ought to make representatives of women's lib quite dizzy. The man's chest and shoulders are padded. His strength appears only in cases where he has eluded woman's sexual avidity and plays the pimp.

Seventeen years after the *Proust* Lindner created his second portrait, that of Marilyn. In between there had been a portrait of Verlaine, a group portrait in which Lindner settled accounts with several contemporaries, and above all, a

portrait of Ludwig II. *Marilyn Was Here* was also preceded by a series of sketches. The portrait was shown for the first time at the Sidney Janis Gallery in New York and was exhibited along with works by Indiana, Allen Jones, Oldenburg, Dali (*Mao-Marilyn*), Warhol, Rosenquist and others. In the catalogue Lindner was the only one to accompany his work with something of an epitaph: "Public Lips." The words can be compared to Eluard's "la rose publique" but they also seem to explain Lindner's painting which goes back to the source of the Marilyn legend, her availability — the star with the childlike voice behaved as her dedicated cult of followers demanded. Lindner's expression might be translated this way: "Lips of the People." What gives the myth such fascination is perhaps the illumination it received after her death. One thinks of James Dean, Katherine Mansfield, Warhol who barely escaped death but was consumed by myth even before his hour came. What led Marilyn towards death was the kiss of the entire world; she had to remain an unchanging symbol, fixed once and for all, a Campbell's soup can that people couldn't stop opening. "She was the symbol of the obsession, typically American, of sex and death. They made her into a little girl and then kept her in the refrigerator." Only that absolute ban on escaping from the nation's nursery could create the fiction of her immortality. Time must not touch the idol. Lindner: "In America people do not admire the legs of an eighty-year old Mistinguette."

In Lindner's work Marilyn is portrayed in a frontal view, a veritable goddess of death, similar to one of those cardboard figures which serve as targets for marines taking rifle practice. The image of a target is a kind of magic symbol of the hunt, American style, and brings to mind the drawings of the prehistoric grottos of Altamira. Defenseless, the opposite of the *Proust*, she is left exposed to every aggression, every assault, every dream. She literally seems to attract them. Like the portrait of Proust, Marilyn's is divided into two halves, one of them death and suffocation, the pulsations of life reduced to mere memory. The head is plunged into darkness. Here Lindner may have been reminded of Picabia's *Nuit espagnole* (1922), a sort of persiflage about a female Saint Sebastian. But by comparing it to the fetishes that usually accompany Lindner's figures, it becomes an attack on the consumer. Lindner is preparing the public image of Marilyn. That is why the corset becomes a terrifying instrument of castration which imposes distance, like Proust's starched collar. Through the homage he pays her, Lindner is the only one to free Marilyn from passivity. He presents her as a poisoned fruit, a new Lulu, Eve and Pandora simultaneously.

WERNER SPIES

The Meeting. *1953. Huile sur toile. (Oil on canvas). 152 x 183 cm. The Museum of Modern Art, New York.*

17

One Afternoon. *1958. Huile sur toile*
(Oil on canvas). 101.5 x 76 cm.
Coll. Denise Lindner. (Photo Cordier
and Ekstrom, New York.)

Ice. *1966. Huile sur toile.*
(Oil on canvas). 178 x 153 cm.
Whitney Museum of American Art,
New York. (Photo Geoffrey Clements.)

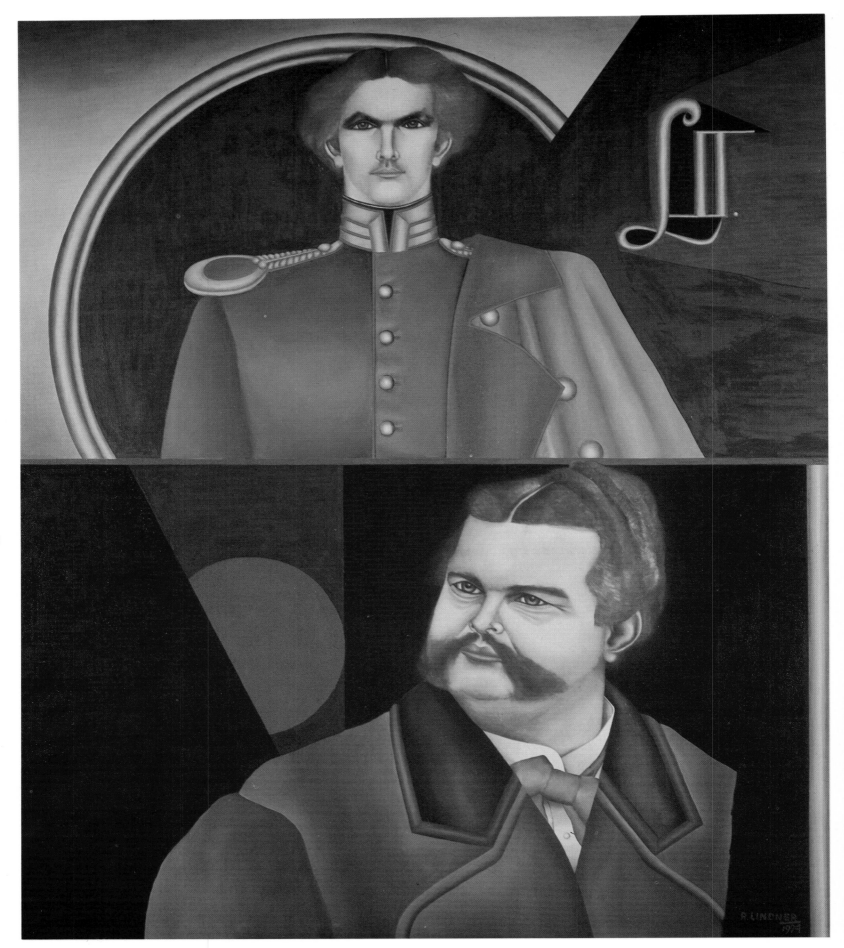

20

Ludwig II. *1974. Huile sur toile (Oil on canvas). 221 x 170.2 cm. (Photo Fisher Fine Arts.)*

Amazone. *1975. Aquarelle et collage sur papier (Watercolor and collage on paper). 54.5 x 41.5 cm. Galerie Maeght, Paris.*

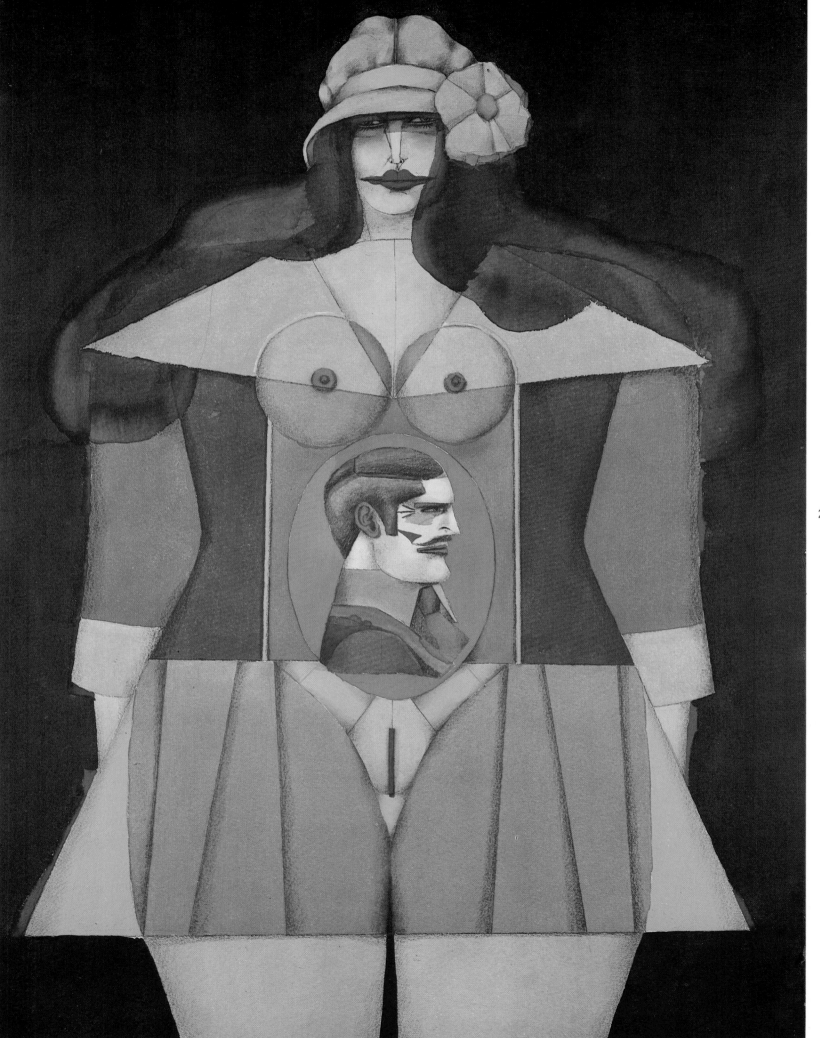

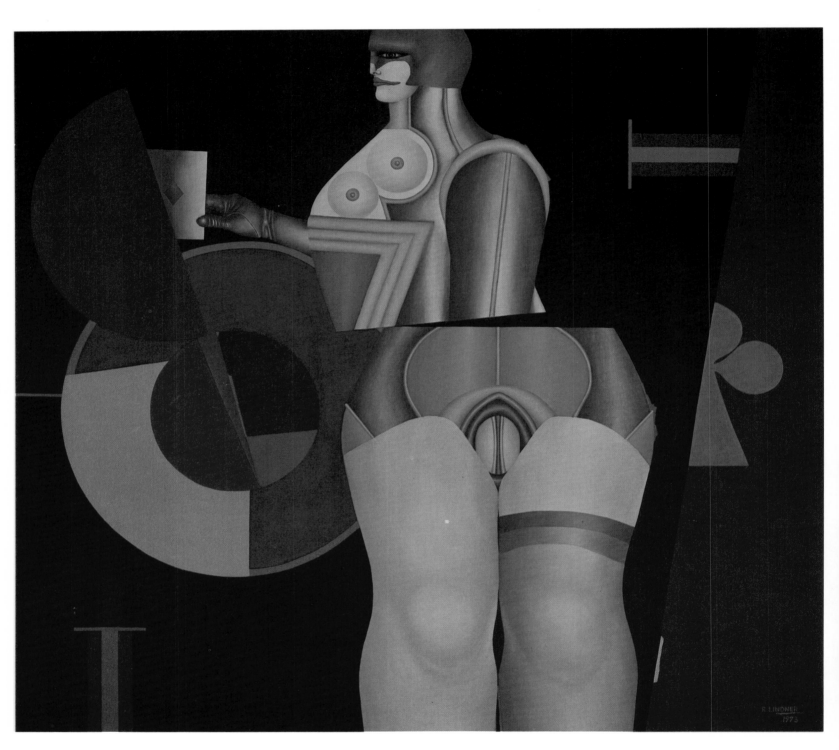

Solitaire. *1973. Huile sur toile*
(Oil on canvas). 200 x 180 cm.
Galerie Marie-Louise Jeanneret—
Art Moderne, Geneva.

The F.B.I. on East 69th Street.
1972. Huile sur toile (Oil on
canvas). 200 x 175 cm. Museum
Boymans-Van Beuningen, Rotterdam.

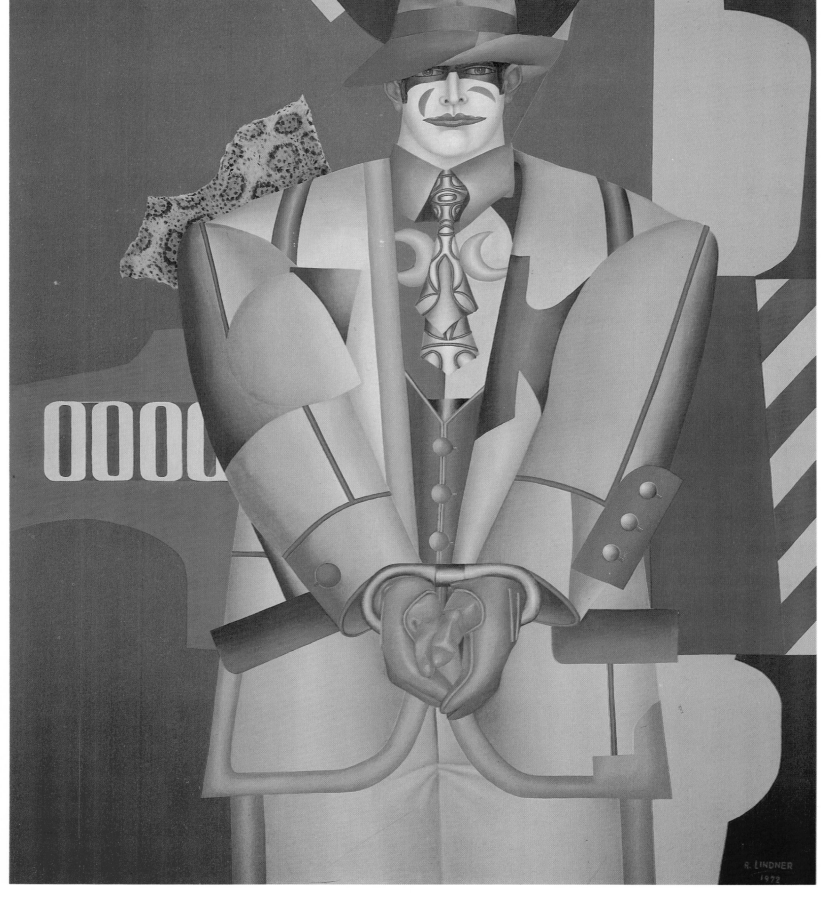

Untitled. *1967. Watercolor*
102 x 72cm. Private collection.
(Photo Galerie Maeght, Saint-
Paul-de-Vence.)

Woman on Yellow Background.
1972. Watercolor. 65 x 44 cm.
Private collection (Photo
Galerie Maeght, Saint-Paul-de-
Vence.)

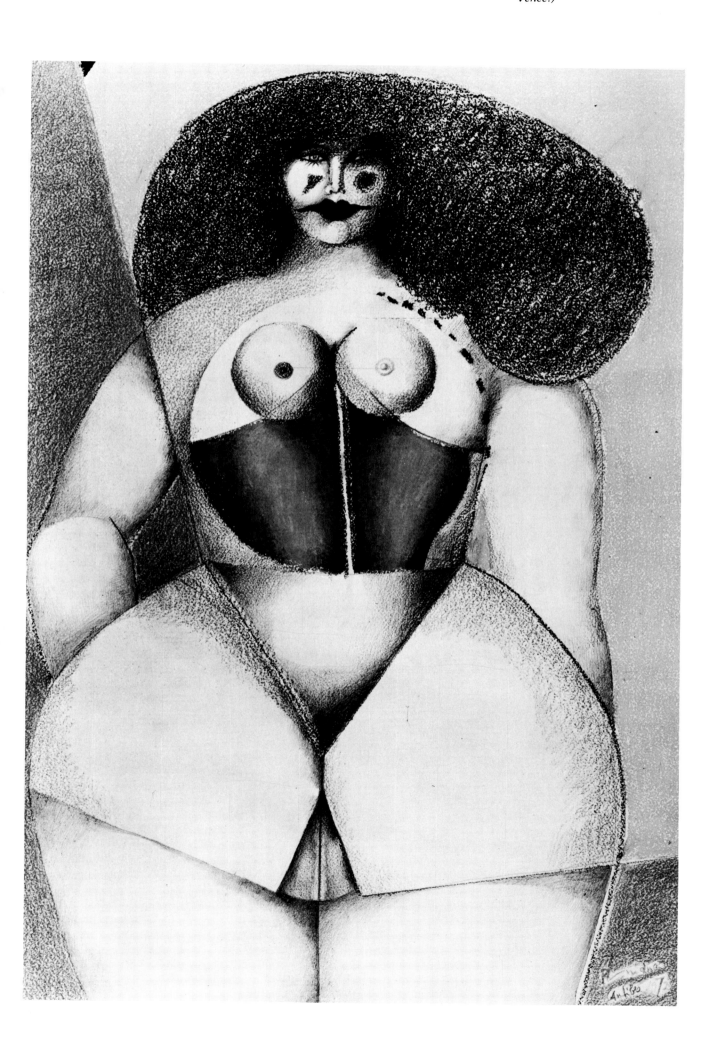

the dragon lady and the supermale or the giotto of the underworld

by pierre volboudt

"Every garment is an emblem." Dr. Diogene Teufelsdrockh's assertion could well serve as an epigraph to Lindner's work. His characters — tightly strapped in the uniforms of an implacable feminity and skeptical dandies, all buttoned up to the chin — seem pinned to the model of a repetitive anatomy, symbols of their sex and their function. The sartorial chic of these debauched creatures posing one after another makes them less what they seem than what they are. Their figures are no more than empty shells, rigid dolls, with wan, painted flesh, modeled and lacquered with wax. With a ruler and T-square, the artist, like the dressmaker, shapes an exclusive and perverse pattern that bears his personal stamp.

The garment conceals and confesses with an insolent immodesty; it displays yet it hides. It takes on all the folds of life. It is the trappings of desire and seduction, the lure that attracts the consenting prey, the ritual uniform, the requisite costume, the disarray that adds a certain grace to the human form. With Lindner, it is the comparison of the human animal, the costume of the male dressed in his Sunday best on the lookout for the alluring female who is prowling about. It is not a question of embellishing, of beautifying, of unveiling, of exalting the graceful body, either the sensual curves, or the virile torso. Skin is no longer the clothing. "Colors undress," said Cendrars. Here nudity, if not forbidden, is offered, but parsimoniously. Sometimes just a slit in a skirt or an unhooked bodice permits a glimpse into nudity. Vamps or bacchantes under their shields, polished pimps and louts, are the fauna in this parade of the inanimate. Each specimen is constructed on the same pattern, bedecked with the same accessories, embellished with drab putty or corseted in a flashy costume and signed by the same worker: Lindner.

The Lindner line, with the exception of a few slight alterations, is marked in all of his creations. The model is set once and for all, in the form of a certain Yankee type, but almost a caricature.

In the squared-off solidity of the canvas, quartered into large sections, the painter blends the disparate influences that have led him to construct the "eternal woman," her features borrowed, perhaps from Kirchner or his emulators, from Otto Dix and Grosz, schematized after the example of Schlemmer for whom the Bauhaus was a sort of remote offshoot of Arezzo. The figures stand together alongside the crowds, the billboards, the neon lights of Broadway, pages of advertising from New York magazines. After Alexander Platz comes West 48th Street. Expressionism, if the term does not conflict with gross vulgarity, provocative extravagance, or the outrageous excesses of the characters, is right there at the tip of his brush, clear and sharp. Lindner exaggerates their get-up to the point of the grotesque; hair is like luxuriant fleece mimicking the false mane of a circus fawn, shoddy fur is seen through the window pane of a bar, or some shabby merchandise sits in the window of the Sankt Pauli district. Constricted in their street finery, with swollen libidos, padded with stuffing, these buxom ruffians are the starched puppets out of the *commedia dell'arte*, absent-minded beings on the abstract stage, who ought to bear a title borrowed from Baudelaire's phrase, "the dangerous and intimate connection between savagery and lust."

It might be said that these figures have been taken down from billboards where their live doubles line up each evening, well-pressed, ready-to-wear beings. Female machines whose charms are symbolic circles and triangles, comical rosettes standing there like targets to resist the arrows, or mechanical male clods with their elegant U.S.A.-made bodies; they are all made of plates fitted to an invisible framework. Slashes and openings, flared skirts pleated into fan shapes, never reveal anything more than a cold lining of metal, smooth and taut, the flesh of an automaton. *The Bride Stripped Bare* is an assemblage of human organs, a diagram of the machinery of desire. With his couples, Lindner, the geometer of sex, constructs conclusive theorems on the mechanized eros. His figures make contact with each other, touch each other, but nearly always tangentially; they feel for each other with awkward glances; body contact is taboo. Even undressing is but the dismantling, piece by piece, by the lonely robot.

The individual is reduced to the function of a clothes rack, a support with a human face. Within this panoply he struts about, with his inflated sense of omnipotence that anonymity confers upon him. He identifies himself with the haunting prototype in which instinct and vice are united. He makes a monstrous fetish out of "the dressed-up, primitive, unvaried uniform of the new world type," which Chateaubriand viewed as the "last garment for future convicts." There is no question of a soul. Under the starched cloth, under the nylon, the individual

Man with Moustache. *1960. Pastel. 34.5 x 30 cm. Mr. and Mrs. Arne H. Ekstrom collection. (Photo Geoffrey Clements.)*

28

Couple. *1969. Watercolor. 142 x 117. Leonard Lauder collection. (Photo Geoffrey Clements).*

Couple II. *1969. Gouache. 61 x 50.5 cm. Private collection. (Photo Galerie Claude Bernard, Paris.)*

becomes a perfect imitation of crumbled sheet metal, like a mechanical toy that moves by springs — nothing more than a stereotype produced by Society.

A disturbing, cold-blooded tragedy seems to emanate from this hypnotic ballet which features the confrontation of the Vanquished Mistress and the Swashbuckler, the Dragon Lady and the Spellbound Supermale, the latter in the process of being vanquished by the veneal Lilith. Like a triumphant idol, she is sure of her evil power, and contemptuously awaits the moment when she will crush her iron bosom against the admirer she has encountered by chance. The woman seems to ignore her prey. Whether he stares at her or turns away, she throws him a glance of indifference; her face is marked by the same expressionless cruelty of an official who stands at the head of some barbarous cult. He, in turn, stands there, with clenched jaws, eyebrows black as coal, a parody of passion. Yet, he has before him only the ridiculous imitation of a body, an impassive giantess whose tapered lips bite instead of delivering the promised kiss. She has traded in her protective armor for a boa constrictor which, like a lasso, will entwine the two adversaries, and then, in this unusual bond, unite them. One of the keys to Lindner's work is certainly this symbolic bestiality. The battle of the sexes is the struggle between two giants, going through motions in their mutual trance, concealing with clichés, their eternal conflict.

The combatants fight with unequal weapons, driven toward each other by the same despotic frenzy that motivates the "struggle for life." Gloves on their fists, these champions in the battle for existence are stars in the painter's American dream. The affectations of the brothel, the debased chic of the saloons — these are the proper settings for his characters, who are, after all, only masks.

Behind the mask, however, there is the supposition that someone else exists — someone who defies, deceives, terrorizes and intrigues. But in Lindner's world, nothing exists beyond that pseudo self; the individual has a functional reality but remains incognito. Lindner's gallery of hes and shes are spectors, endowed with flesh, but dehumanized actors in a nightmarish carnival. Under their intense frigidity, their inexorable passivity, they celebrate the saturnalia of licentiousness according to their programmed masochistic natures.

The game seems to be regulated in accordance with some ritual and the hand is played out in advance, as if the deck were stacked. Each of the artist's figures is like a player waiting for an opponent to lay down his hand. But how can the high card be bluffed? The ace is always in the hands of the queen of spades, the maiden holding the sword, the female executioner in her hellish outfit, who looks at her

Woman and Handbag. *1964.*
Pencil and gouache.
73.5 x 58.5 cm. (Photo
Galerie Claude Bernard,
Paris.)

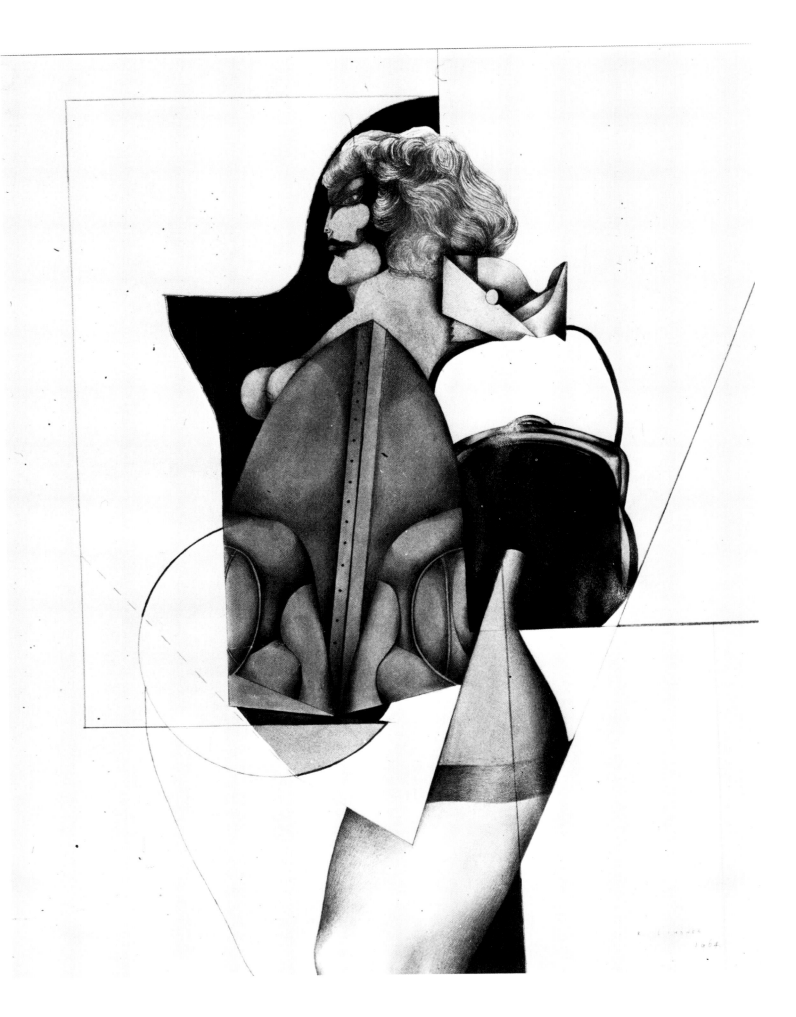

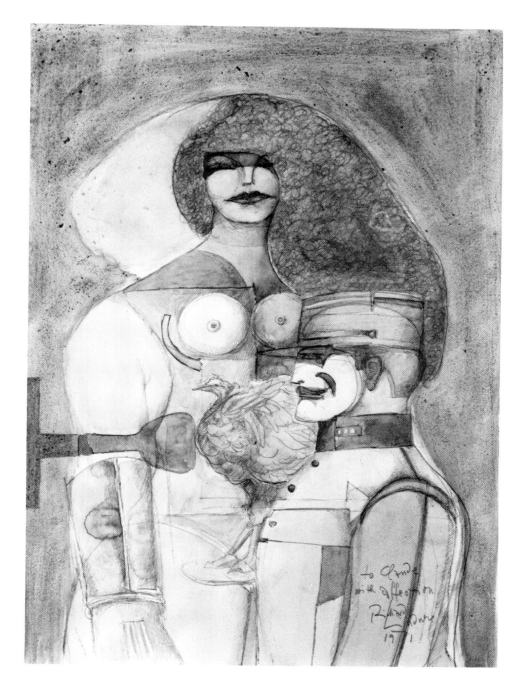

enterprising partner, and with a prophetic gesture, gives him notice of his defeat and excludes him from the game.

Without equivocating, this parable is the most brutal. Art, through its solemn simplification, helps the painter serve the parable. There is an element of the primitive here — an intense, sharply brilliant rite, without any nuances, a rite that is carried out in a formal, sacred manner. Bound by the stifling and strangling iron collar, clothed in an ornamental necklace, Lindner's characters seem seized in a sort of ecstasy which lifts them out of their sordid banality to the level of timeless myths.

An oblique eye, drawn toward the temple, sees and sees not. The passerby is fascinated, attracted to the promises of Pandora — the timeless Eve.

Giotto, whom Lindner professed to admire, would probably not have rejected his spontaneous and profane disciple. The legend of Scrovegni of Padua would also serve as impious blashpemy for these heroines who are always on their guard with the slogan: "Noli me tangere" (don't touch). All things being equal, shouldn't Lindner be considered the Giotto of the underworld?

Pierre Volboudt

Untitled. *1971. Watercolor. 30 x 44 cm. (Photo Galerie Claude Bernard, Paris.)*

a political biographical approach to a life between three worlds:

Hitler in 1921.
(Photo Lapi-Viollet.)

Fischer:

Yesterday was July 20th, twenty-nine years after the failed attempt on Hitler's life in 1944, an event that concerns another generation and yet a new book has just appeared that has been a great success: "Have You Seen Hitler?"[2] I ask you the same question: Have you seen Hitler?

Lindner:

I saw Hitler every day in Munich at the Café Heck, a small café with about ten tables and thirty seats. It doesn't exist anymore. When I was in Munich three years ago I asked around but nobody had heard of the Café Heck. However, Hitler used to sit there everyday at his usual table. Our table was beside his and we knew each other because we avoided direct contact. At the time his loyal supporters were there with him — Strasser and Goering too. Goebbels rarely came from Berlin. This happened during the years 1929-1933. Then I had to leave Germany quickly. I always found Hitler to be the sort of fellow who pleased young maidens. He was a romantic, in the petty bourgeois sense of the word — a romantic for dressmakers. He dressed in black, with a black artist's hat, black suit, black tie; he often wore high boots, riding boots and carried a whip in his hand. But he was very shy. He never dared make a spectacle of himself whereas others were a good deal noisier, Hess, for example. Hitler was always careful to make a good impression, to appear as a good bourgeois among the people of this café…and he always wanted to be with artists.

He knew that you were an artist?

Yes, of course. At the time I was very well known in Munich. I was always at my usual table with friends from "Simplicissimus" — Karl Arnold, Gulbransson, Heine — all of whom knew Hitler very well. Of course, they heaped insults on him, but with impunity; Hitler never dared to reply to the artists or say anything whatsoever to them. Respect for the artists! In the evening he often went to their restaurant, the Austria-Bavaria, for example. He was the type who delighted maids since he was exactly their kind of hero.

So meeting Hitler was not a nightmare at first?

Yes, yes, it was a nightmare intellectually! The man put on this bourgeois manner and took special care to make everything seem in order — a carefully knotted tie, the refinement and behavior of a distinguished man — a fellow who appeals to maids! Hitler had remarkably beautiful, slender and delicate hands. However, he had the look of a simpleton, a romantic, as if he were incapable of doing anything.

All the same, wasn't he terrifying from the very beginning?

Yes, yes, when he spoke. I often heard him; no, not often, perhaps three times. Yes, he was a

europe, america, and the no-man's land of emigration statements by wolfgang georg fischer[1]

Ruins of the Cloister of Messines, Dec. 1914. Watercolor of Adolf Hitler. Viollet collection.

real terror. He used to shout hysterically.

Who was the most nightmarish character from your childhood and your youth — your father, Richard Wagner, your professor of religion, Bismarck, Wotan or your professor at the Munich Academy? Who, as far as you can recollect, stands out as the nightmarish character?

What's interesting about that question is that I've never asked it of myself, though I'm past seventy and faced with it. I have to say that I have transformed all the nightmarish characters who used to haunt me into something — a drawing or a figure of my imagination, the imagination of a young man who frequently went out alone, accompanied only by his imagination even though he knew many people. The things I observed which terrified me later I have also transposed, you may say in a creative way, but I wasn't the creator.

The first teacher who slapped you — do you remember him?

From start to finish, yes. They all terrorized me. In my generation teachers were nightmarish, not the sort you could trust, not father figures. All the children felt the way I did, not just me. All the young people, from the gymnasium to the lycée.

Isn't that true for every child with natural, artistic talent? Did your teacher ever say: You have no right to draw, you have to do mathematics; or making music is not permitted, you'd do better studying history?

It was just the opposite for me. They all said: You don't have to do mathematics, just draw. That was nice. But the teacher by virtue of his profession was a nightmarish character.

And the first teacher at the Academy, the one who you told me made everyone sit down one day in rows?

A funny character out of a bad play. Imagine a room with four or five artists and the professor, a sort of "Professor Unrat,"[3] except that he claimed to be an artist. He wasn't a nightmarish character; we weren't afraid of him. We

Panorama of Munich from the
tower of the city hall.
(Photo Harungue-Viollet.)

34

Were you in Munich at that time?

Yes, but it was all a failure. Everything I saw was a failure, including Hitler. I saw how he fled from the Feldherrnhalle in 1923. That too was a failure! In Bavaria everything failed!

No nightmarish characters there?

Yes. The S.A. I didn't know the S.S. I had already left. The S.A. wasn't entirely nightmarish because we were still there with our force, the Social Democratic Party. We did a good job of beating each other up. If the S.A. stopped one of us who happened to be out alone, that person was out of luck; and vice-versa. The S.A. had already become a hateful apparition. But the truly redoubtable character I read about later, when I was in Paris.

Read?

Yes, yes. I was here in Paris. In 1933 I left Germany. I spent no more than a single day in Germany after the Nazis took over.

And who was this nightmarish character? The new Hitler?

The new Hitler, the one who was truly in power. Hitler frightened us because he was Austrian. Had he been German we would have known a lot of things about him.

Was he in some way an enigma?

Yes, an enigma. There is something very important about that. Next there was the great event: Hitler came to Munich because he had been imprisoned there. He stayed there because it was a city of art, because the architecture of Italian classicism appealed to him.

In your universe of irony, scorn and deeper meaning [4] hidden beneath a clown's suit, are there also some positive figures? Someone whom you appreciated and admired?

That goes back too far to talk about here.

For example, an historical character who impressed you?

Yes, there were people who impressed me like Kafka and Proust. In music, Schöenberg who at that time was for me the Freud of music. In general we didn't know too much about Freud. I knew of his existence, but any bookseller today knows more about Freud than we did then.

Was there someone about whom you wondered: will I some day be able to do the same?

Yes. Picasso, towards the end of his cubist period. Cubist reproductions had just appeared.

Picasso up to 1920?

Up to 1925. When I was a student, an advanced student, I had in my studio a rather large reproduction of *Three Musicians*, which I had picked up somewhere; anyway, it caused a great stir among my professors. But as I said, reproductions were not readily available. There

laughed, not under his nose, but afterwards... However, I really believe he was a bit nightmarish anyhow. You're right, since he had the power to show people the door. He could have taken revenge on us but to my knowledge he never did.

He never destroyed a painting?

He would never have done that. It was contrary to the Academy's program. He had to produce a certain result and a certain number of works. Each of us had to do so many nudes, so many of this, so many of that.

Your father, was he a nightmarish character, in the Freudian sense?

No, on the contrary. My father was a nice man whom I loved, but he was a coward. He shifted responsibility for everything on to my mother and that made her an imposing figure.

Then, wasn't she a nightmarish character?

No, my god, she wasn't very intelligent, a very Wagnerian woman, physically too — with a bust! People find her here and there in my paintings.

Any other nightmarish characters? A gestapo agent? A soldier?

The army didn't frighten me since it was very far away. I was too young to serve in the war, the first war, and then I only knew revolutions — unsuccessful revolutions, to tell the truth.

would be only a little book and basta! that was it.

But Tannhauser in Munich had already exhibited him?

Yes, he had shown Picasso, but I have to tell you this: we weren't really going into the galleries; there we were — all against art! It was when Dadaism was winding down. We students were always a bit behind, especially in Munich, which was truly provincial where art was concerned. The myth about Munich being a city of art is absolute nonsense. The average level has always been low. At the Academy, for example, there was always a crowd of bad painters. The Glaspalast was pathetic. There was practically no art in Munich, only a bourgeois type of art.

And Kandinsky and his friends?

That was before my time. That crowd was ten or fifteen years older than I.

When did you first run into anti-Semitism? How and where?

To tell the truth, I didn't notice much anti-Semitism, neither at school nor at the Academy. In Bavaria, anti-Semitism arrived with Hitler.

But before, throughout your life, an experience from childhood? "I am a Jew." That must have happened to you. "I am different...there are various problems that make me different."

Yes, but first of all, I always found that it was others who are different, not me. I grew up in a nonpracticing family. We knew that we were Jewish but, well, we didn't make an occupation out of it. Besides, I was invited everywhere so I never noticed. In intellectual circles, young intellectuals in speaking of Jews were always very positive...truthfully, I had no encounters with anti-Semitism before the Nazis...

Do you recall the personal resonance that certain "great days" of recent history had for you? How are they reflected in your everyday life? The day the first world war ended, the day Hitler took power in 1933, the first day of your emigration?

I remember that at school there was a yearly celebration of the king's birthday.

The Wittelsbach?

Yes, the Wittelsbach. I had to sing but I didn't know the words. I had a teacher who was very nasty and who knew I didn't know the words. He planted himself in front of me and stared, focusing on my lips, and I — I had to pretend. It was the hymn "Heil unserer König..."[5] or whatever. And at no time did he turn his eyes away from me. It is surprising since he was a young professor.

A young sadist!

A young sadist, a future Nazi probably. I had friends who became Nazis. They informed on Jews. I have to be explicit about this, those same people who insisted that I return to Germany and who told me: you will be fabulously well treated...

After 1933?

After 1933! But that hymn played an important role. It was the first time that I was forced to be a patriot, physically. Left truly an indelible impression I assure you. I was perhaps seven years old...a memory as indelible as the time Hitler came to power. Most of the time I used to go to the movies twice a day because it was dark inside the cinema and I had some peace. Don't screw around. That was my ideal. Don't screw around. Not doing anything ought to take place in the dark where you don't get a bad conscience from doing nothing since you can't really do anything there. So I was going to the movies twice a day, and one day I came out of the theatre and Hitler was in power. It was in the afternoon, around two o'clock.

In Munich?

In Munich. That evening there was a great torchlight parade. I couldn't go back to my house because I knew they were already there to arrest me. It wasn't a question of my Jewishness but of my politics. I turned around and around. I had to join my wife one way or another. I beat it during the night.

You didn't have a telephone?

All the lines had already been tapped. I knew I was on the list. So I jumped into a taxi. At the time taxis were like the English taxis of today. You were seated very high up and behind a window glass. The torchlight parade was a surprise to the inhabitants of Munich: it was improvised. My taxi entered the parade — to the right and to the left there were S.A. carrying torches. I was seated there in the taxi, holding my nose because of my profile. I knew, of course, what it would look like if a torch were shined on the inside of the car. I would be a shadow and that shadow would be that of a Shylock with a nose! We moved very slowly. Sometimes we had to wait. My fear grew. In the taxi I got closer to where I lived. I wanted to catch a glimpse of my wife in passing. I succeeded but not completely. We had agreed beforehand that both of us would have to slip away. But she wasn't on the list and was able to leave one or two days later. Finally, it happened that even with my Shylock profile we accompanied the parade, very slowly, often having to halt as is usual with parades. And the torches made my shadow even more pronounced. That, if you like, was my worst experience with the Nazis.

You spend a large part of the year here in Paris, your wife is French, but you are also a New Yorker, fascinated by Manhattan. However, you still love the symbol of your Bavarian childhood — Leberknödelsuppe,[6] you recognize it. If people called you a German-American painter, would you take that as a reproach or as something accurate?

I wear the label in any case because my characters give the impression of tourists arriving in New York. I am the only person who paints like this in America. I don't belong to any movement, not to pop art or to any other. I am a tourist who visits America and who sees everything. Saul Steinberg and I have a lot in common in this respect. We are both tourists; we arrived here under very similar conditions; we are friends; and naturally we see New York a lot better than someone who was born here. I am a tourist everywhere, I mean, an observer.

You have often told me that museums don't offer you anything and that other painters' paintings could be stolen from you. But what then are the subjects that stimulate you? The people you see passing in the street, the stores, fashion photographs?

The things that occupy us every day. The subjects that really interest me are the little things in life that I seek to symbolize. Fundamentally, I am interested in the waiting room.

The waiting room of the doctor, the lawyer, the...

No, the waiting room of life. We are all in a waiting room. We are awaiting death. When you're young, you don't think about it much; when you're older, you think about it more; it's really a waiting room. We have to spend our time doing something. That's why they invented business and I don't know what else, just to keep busy. Otherwise you stay seated there and wait for the day when you kick the bucket. There it is, that's my way of looking at it. As a philosophy it's a bit crude and perhaps naive, but in the main, without going into detail, I would say, yes, it's the waiting room that interests me.

I would say that in the waiting room I look at Rembrandts or Vermeers.

Yes, certainly. I don't mean that if there is a book there on Rembrandt I won't look at it, but ultimately...and first of all that's the way it is, a man who creates, whether he writes or paints, looks at others who do the same only to get something from them.

Or else he looks at what others are getting from him.

In any case we don't look at a painting as others do. We don't read a book like just anyone. I look at a painting as a painter. So when I need help I tend to look sideways at another painter. It happens very rarely but the older I get the more I make the mistake of thinking that I don't need any help. But we are all looking at each other a bit. We read books, we listen to what is said because we do need help.

But the typical museum goer is also looking for help, human not professional assistance.

Yes, there are a lot of reasons for going there and these don't interest us. We don't go to the museum just to go to the museum; besides, I think older people need less assistance.

In all respects?

In all respects. Curiosity — one ought not to say that we aren't curious. Every person who creates is curious up until his death — curiosity moves around. I have a lot of detestable ideas about creating which is why I don't feel too comfortable. For example, I think that our signature, we...

Overvalue it?

No, we have a steady need for it. I paint Lindners and you write Fischers. When people say of an artist: "He has found himself," I found it very pitiful.
but he already has his stamp, his signature. Over the years we all become restricted by the signature.

Fundamentally, you are saying that you are afraid of the lack of freedom that is established as soon as we say: That's Chaplin. Chaplin isn't allowed to walk straight.

I think that what's sad in a man's life is his finding a label. Everyone from the greatest to the

37

Sir Henry Irving in the role of Shylock from Shakespeare's "Merchant of Venice."

The Resistble Ris of Arturo
By Bertolt Brecht

38

Drawing for the poster
The Resistible Ascension of Arthur VI. *1968. Museum of Art, Rhode Island School of Design.*

not so great: a signature. One becomes a Fischer or a Lindner, one works at becoming a somebody.

In fact, you have to be a Proteus?

Yes. We are put in a certain position in society by our signature: it's a Picasso...! If it is discovered that it is by someone they don't recognize, someone of the second rank, they say: this is bad, very bad.

Yes, since the Renaissance that has been the mark of individualism. Four hundred years of European culture has produced this.

That's what they worked for, but all of them have become signatures. Well, not all. Michelangelo was always Michelangelo, with or without his signature.

What in your life has most given you wings? Your freedom, the company of good friends, women, travels, wealth, or finally, art?

My greatest adventure has been New York. Women are very important to me, that hasn't changed. Only I have changed. For me men are a pathetic business because women are stronger. It has always been like that.

I would like to ask you one last question which follows from an hypothesis: if you had a choice between the life of a court painter, with Gonzago in Mantua or somewhere in northern Italy, and the life of a leader of an avant-garde artistic revolution, which would you choose?

That's a good question. I am going to tell you the truth in a different way. If I were given the legion of honor or the rosette, I would gladly wear it, but I don't believe in it because I am a painter. That's a truthful answer.

Remember the salon painters believed in it and were enthusiastic about it.

But I'm just not interested. The truth is that Duchamp too would gladly have worn the rosette if he had been able to.

I understand.

That's the answer. We all have a dual personality. We want to be avant-garde and a good bourgeois at the same time. Here they often call me "maître". It's awful. I have a special pin. I'm a member of the American Academy of Arts and Letters, a sort of imitation of the Académie Française. A lot of French people belong to it. Whenever I put on my pin in front of the mirror, I'm appalled. The decoration makes me look ten years older. When you're young they don't give it to you; when you're old you can't wear it anymore because it makes you look old. Yesterday, I put it on to buy the apartment I showed you...

Quai Voltaire?

Yes, there were photos of Pétain inside. We were very anxious to have the apartment and the people were only very polite at first. I said to

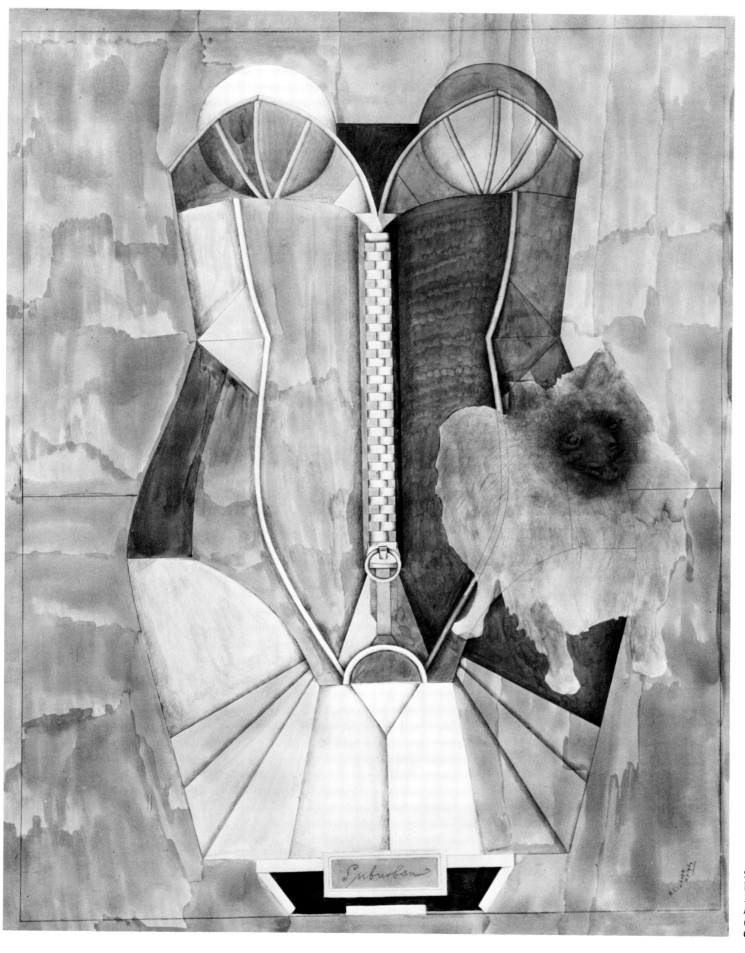

Suburban. *1969.*
Watercolor. 150 x
115 cm. Galerie
Maeght, Paris.
(Photo Geoffrey
Clements.)

New York City II. *1964.*
Watercolor and pencil.
73.5 x 58 cm. Kalamazoo
Institute of Arts, Michigan.

Woman with Hat. *1964. Water-*
color and pencil. 76 x 102 cm.
(Photo Galerie Maeght, Saint-
Paul-de-Vence.)

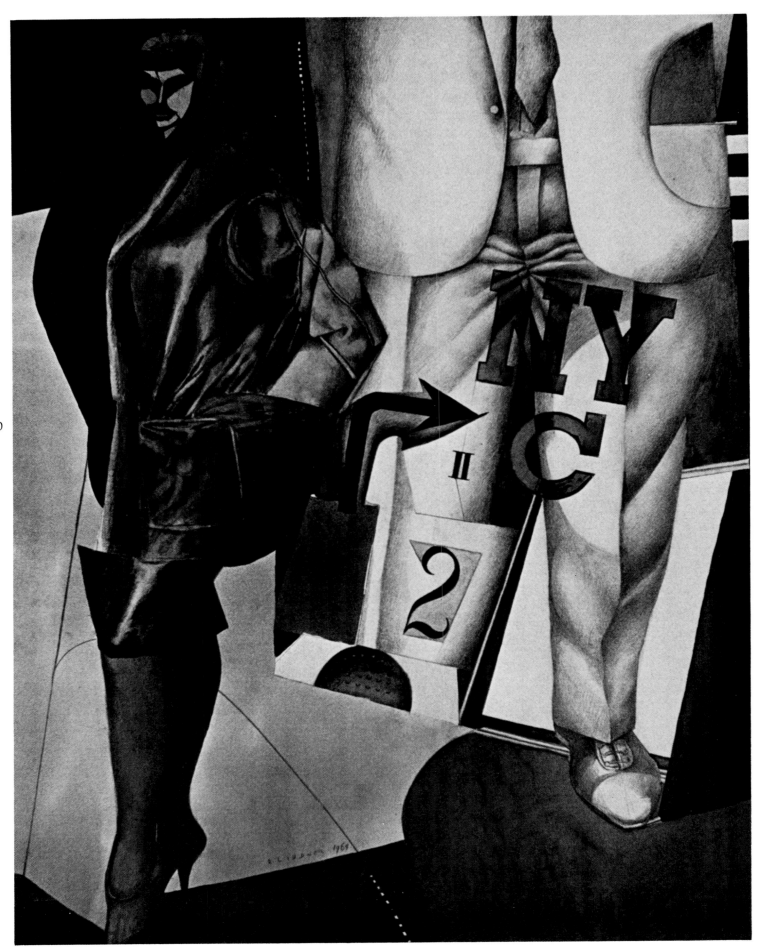

Couple. *1955. Huile sur toile*
(Oil on canvas). 127 x 152 cm.
Coll. particulière, U.S.A.

42

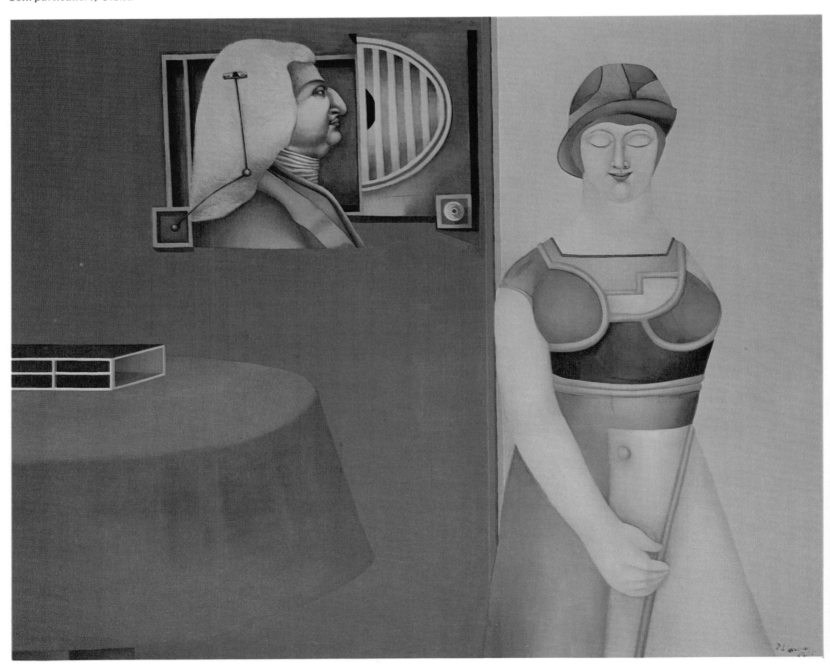

Kiss. *1969. Aquarelle sur papier. (Watercolor). 61 x 51 cm. Coll. Nancy Schwartz, New York. (Photo Galerie Maeght, Saint-Paul-de-Vence.)*

43

Pillow and Almost a Circle. *1969.*
Aquarelle sur papier (Watercolor).
61 x 51 cm. Coll. particulière.
New York. (Photo Galerie Maeght,
Saint-Paul-de-Vence.)

44

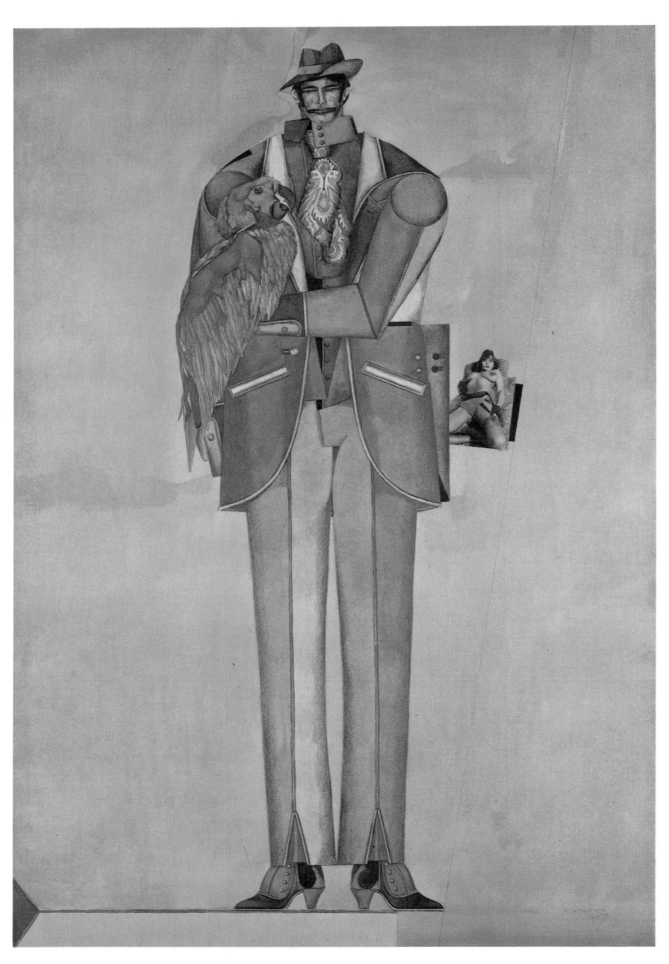

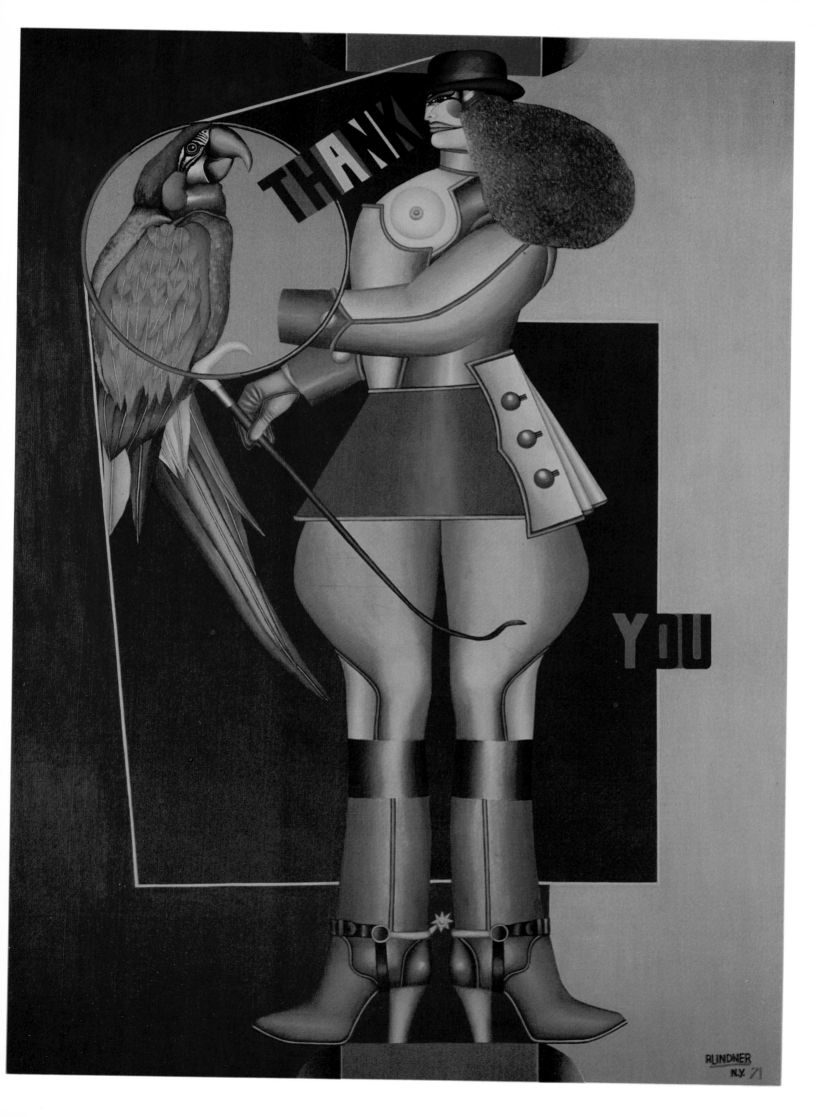

48

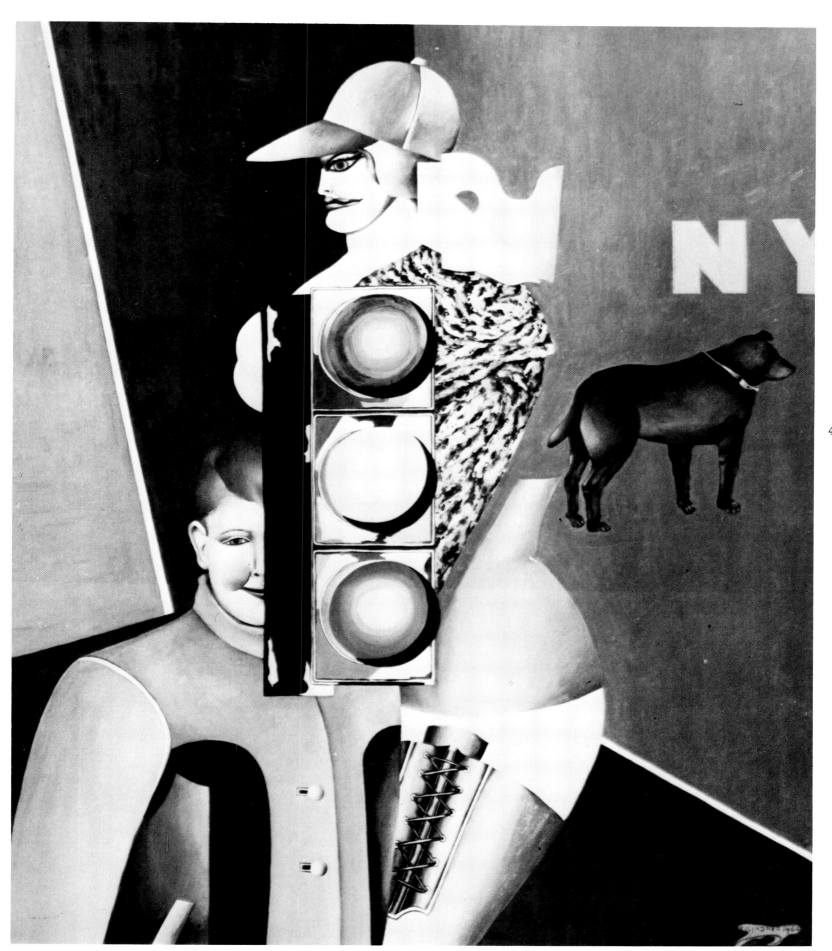

Poet. 1969. Watercolor.
60.7 x 50.2 cm. Private collection, New York. (Photo Fisher
Fine Art Ltd. London.)

Coney Island II. 1964. Oil on
canvas. 178 x 127 cm. Cordier
and Ekstrom collection. (Photo
Geoffrey Clements.)

50

myself: I'm going to wear this dohickey. I put it on and immediately everything changed. But immediately! "Maître", they said and everything turned out for the best.

With the notary or the concierge?

Neither, with the owner. It was like night and day. And then I lost my pin. I thought I didn't want it anymore but when I returned to New York I called at once and asked for a new one...you never know...

The Dadaist uplifted, to put it ironically!

Is that irony? Isn't it really reality? I'm a very disconcerting character at heart. I'm an old man but really I'm a young man — it's true — and not just a young man, a child in a lot of ways, more or less a child of ten or twelve. Everything that is extravagant interests me. I'm serious.

Me too!

But you are still young. For you nothing has changed yet. From now on you can prepare your whole life. There are neither grown-ups or wise people. We always do the same thing over and over more or less. I am doing just about the same thing I was doing when I was little, the same mistakes, the same errors. Everything stays the same, nothing changes. Naturally, it is even more noticeable when you haven't any status. We haven't any status — none. Every normal bourgeois has achieved status by the age of thir-

ty or forty or fifty. Whereas we grow up without having any, like children.

You would have had it as a court painter!

I don't want it but I do perhaps want a studio. In what concerns me I have never bluffed in that respect. Yes, this is what I always said to my students, what I always did. It's also the only way to survive. When you lie that makes troubles for you at once. Picasso, for example, never lied. Picasso was always himself..Balthus was an aristocrat. He paints like an aristocrat and not like a painter...If you give a brush to an aristocrat he tends to paint the same type of paintings. He paints honestly, what he wants to.

A propos of honesty — and Léger. And communist symbolism?

He wasn't a communist. I knew him. He was a loyal man and his subject was the proletariat. He had very little in common with proletarians, however. He was an intellectual. What did Picasso have to do with communism? Yes, we are all traitors, people who cannot be counted on. We constantly change our way of thinking, depending on the role we find ourselves in. A role that is agreeable today may not be so tomorrow. For example, when I make a mistake like the one I made yesterday.

What mistake?

I used a transparent red.

Collection of Richard Lindner's toys. (Photo Piotr Trawinski.)

Collection of Richard Lindner's Indian art. (Photo Piotr Trawinski.)

51

On the painting "The Ace of Clubs"?

The shirt is red. I was careless and used a transparent color and then spent the entire day removing it. If you interviewed me yesterday, I would have been upset. Today, I've removed the red and the situation is again different. I don't believe a word of what a creator says. The ones who are good for nothing have their principles, the mediocre have a solid way of seeing, a solid philosophy. I have discovered that the men who are truly creators are traitors, liars, people who cannot be relied upon.

WOLFGANG GEORG FISCHER

Paris, July 21, 1973

1. W. G. Fischer, born in Vienna in 1933 of a Jewish family, has published two novels — *Wohnungen*, 1960, and *Möblierte Zimmer*, 1972.
2. Walter Kempowsky, *Haben sie Hitler Gesehen?* (Munich, 1973).
3. Professor Unrat: "Professor Garbage" — a ridiculous and pitiful character in Heinrich Mann's novel *The Blue Angel*, which was made into the famous film by Josef von Sternberg.
4. An allusion to the play by Christian Dietrich Grabbe, *Scherz, Satire, Ironie, und tiefere Bedeutung*, 1881.
5. Long live the king!
6. A soup made with liver meatballs.

information about planet lindner

by gilbert lascault

ON THE EXISTENCE
OF PICTORIAL PLANETS

Certain painters (not all) prompt us to become delirious, or tell us more or less disjointed stories, or help us conceive of worlds different from the one in which our daily life unfolds. Compared to their paintings, the worlds of most science fiction writers are somewhat simplistic and systematic.

Painting is a subtle act. It evades the trap of definition. It rejects the constraints of grammar. It allows for our ecstasies and our accounts of ourselves, guides them and leaves them free of barriers. It is always simultaneously both above and beyond the theories and fictions we tack on to the works. If we wish to imagine that a painter's works provide information about a strange planet that is all his own, we do so at our own risk and peril, but not without deriving a sense of pleasure. This pleasure is one of the manifold delights that painting gives us.

Therefore, we can assume that pictorial planets exist: an uncertain existence lacking the requisite rapport with the method of each painter and with his intentions. On the Planet

The Gambler. *1951. Oil on canvas. 76 x 66 cm. Saul Steinberg collection, New York.*

52

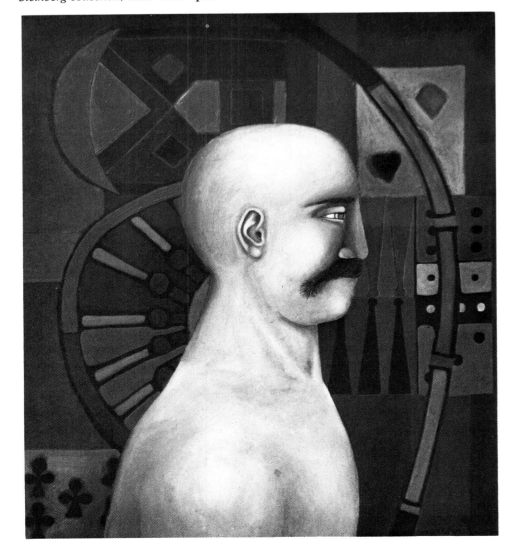

Goya, bulls would fly and giants would devour their sons. On one of the planets of the Constellation Klee, we would encounter aquatic parks, over-sized vegetables, suffering fruits and limp balls of wool. Governed by the Bird Superior and the Woman with a Hundred Heads, Ernst's Planet would be one of tricky planes, non-Euclidean flies and schools of herring. Colorful beings would inhabit Planet Rothko. In this pictorial Milky Way there would also be Planet Miro, Planet Steinberg and many others. Planet Lindner would be full of violence and secrets.

INFORMATION 1: ON THE BESTIARY

DOCUMENTS: *The Meeting* (1953), *Hello* (1966), *Man with a Parrot* (1967), *Thank You* (1971), *A Friend* (1969), *And Eve* (1971), *East 69th Street* (1972), *Leopard Lily* (1966), *Skirt Open* (1966), *42nd Street* (1964).

On Planet Lindner there would be giant cats scarcely smaller than a man and placid cats whose eyes would gleam with a contained ferocity. These cats would enjoy sitting down before a woman in a red dress so that their fur would appear more striking... With their raucous chattering the parrots would make the poets despair although their brilliant colors would make painters rejoice. When a woman would telephone, a serious parrot would perch himself next to her. The bird's belly would have the same coloring as the woman's bra and boots; the red head of the bird would bring to mind a woman's red lips and the heel of her boot. If a man with a small head wore a tie with a complicated design, a jealous parrot would come and perch on his arm, his complex plumage competing with the male's coquetry. Another parrot would converse with a horsewoman in spurs and holding a riding crop but without a left hand. The bird would have eaten her hand; but she would not resent him for it and would look at him with the blank gaze that is characteristic of men and women from there... Also, they would often have dogs near them. They would think that communication is easier between a dog and a human being than between a man and a woman... Several women would have tamed big snakes. They would have taught them how to sleep on their shoulders, to suck their nipples with their bifurcated tongues. New York Eves, Brooklyn Salammbos, they would experience silent pleasure from the cold feel of the reptiles... We would not see living beasts although they would undoubtedly exist on the planet. Tailors would sew coats for men from tiger skins and accessories for women from those of a leopard. A mouth full of teeth of some animal would appear, drawn on a woman's silk panties or on a slot machine. Perhaps, chased by gunshots, the beasts would have disappeared from the planet, leaving only their furs and the memory of their fierce smile: a smile full of teeth.

INFORMATION 2: FASCINATION WITH CIRCLES

DOCUMENTS: *Woman* (1970), *Hello* (1966), *Napoleon Still Life* (1962), *The Secret* (1960), *The Billiard* (1954-55), *Thank You* (1971), *Partners* (1971), *The Visitor* (1953), *Leopard Lily* (1966), *And Eve* (1971), *Boy* (1954), *Couple* (1969), *No* (1966), *Shoot* (1969), etc.

According to certain explorers, Planet Lindner would be inhabited by a strange cult of the circle. But these explorers would quickly prove to be poor witnesses and deplorable observers. First of all there are no religious cults on Planet Lindner. It is an atheistic universe, an irreligious world, without faith in or nostalgia for religion. Ideas of transcendence and of reverence would be both insignificant and senseless there. Space, filled with massive flesh, unpliable fabrics, machines, violent colors and constant barriers would not allow any empty area for the introduction of a soul or religion.

There would be something more serious: the circle, by its mathematical definition and metaphysical metaphors to which it lends itself, would not exist on Planet Lindner. But there would be a multiplicity of rings.

Sometimes the rings would constitute targets. Their colored surfaces would evoke both the geometrical lights of Robert Delaunay and the shooting galleries of carnivals. Aim at the forehead of Ludwig II and the forehead of Wittelsbach who has the sun in his head. Aim at the hip of the telephone operator who has the sun on her hip. Aim at the target located on the left of the lonely woman but don't touch her. Aim at the red of the tricolored cockade as large as Napoleon's head and placed to the right of such a head. If you aim well, hold the rifle and fire a shot at the center of the target, you might activate the image as happens in a traveling show; the woman would then put down her playing card, Napoleon would wink and a Valkyrie would take off her corset. These would be the diversions on this planet.

Other circles would be three-dimensional: buttons in low-relief (so important in Lindnerian apparel), round female breasts in high relief, the roundness of apples, handles of canes, children's heads shaped like balloons. On Planet Lindner the quality of roundness would often define the ideal human body: the roundness of the face, breasts, buttocks, knees; the nearly circular oval that certain feminine garments require around the sex organs. A preference for the circular form would be encountered elsewhere in other universes: Planet Willi Baumeister, Planet Oskar Schlemmer.

Lindnerian rings would sometimes be indications of movement, metallic, with rays such as mechanical instruments: wheels, flywheels, spherical counterweights. The machines would turn incessantly, causing an identical situation to come up at regular intervals. The fascination with the circular would be a result of this reappearing situation that excludes anything else. In this world revolution would mean rotation rather than explosion.

Other rings, perhaps the most troubling in this world, would establish a curious complicity with emptiness. These constitute a manner of encompassing air, of situating a void. There would be the hoop placed near a girl (*Girl*, 1955); another (green, orange, blue and yellow) with which the woman with the red hair is playing (*No*, 1966); the hoop that a little girl in a sailor's outfit is holding while the visitor approaches but

The Visitor. *1953. Oil on canvas. 127 x 76. Miss Mary Harding collection, New York.*

Couple. *1961. Oil on canvas. 94 x 63 cm. Galerie Claude Bernard, Paris.*

gadgets, certain parts of which would be very sturdy and heavy while others would be obviously fragile. Yes, operating a powerful machine might depend on a weak cord. Yes, women would use cord to lace up their corsets while impressing a series of X's on their white skin.

INFORMATION 4: ON LIBERTINE COMMUNITIES

DOCUMENTS: *Couple* (1977), *Encounter* (1976), *Contact* (1977), etc.

On this planet numerous small erotic societies, libertine communities, would submit to arbitrary, detailed rules. If the woman were wearing a blue melon-shaped hat decorated with a violet ribbon, the man would be accompanied by a dog and would wear a gray cap decorated with thin red stripes. If the woman's hat were red, the man's would be purple. And if she dons a purple one, then he ought to wear a gray hat with a yellow ribbon. If a gigantic beige beret forms a halo around the face of a woman with gloves, the man beside her will be much smaller in size, bareheaded and with rouged cheeks. He will wear short gray pants resembling the sheetmetal pipes painted by Fernand Léger.

In a general way, the contract that unites these libertine men and women compels them to use makeup. Their lips must be blue, violet or a harsh bloody red. Their hair could be pink, orange or green, maybe brown, provided that this was not their natural color. The blue of the lips on a masculine face must have as its corollary deep green makeup around the eyes. Certain women match their mauve lips to a subdued mauve dress or to the color of their genitals concealed by the dress.

Close perhaps to the Planet Baudelaire and far from Planet Sade, Planet Lindner would be located near makeup and not near scarification and torture. In libertine communities people avoid humiliating one another or casting aspersions on another's body. Aggression is avoided, not for moral reasons, but because it is seen as behavior that lacks subtlety. Every libertine, every dandy of Eros, endeavors to strike a balance between contact and distance, between provocation and rupture. Every person tries to establish some kind of paradoxical balance upon meeting another. Various delights or rather imperceptible emotions concealed by an affectation of indifference would come out of these balances; in that world these emotions would be considered the most interesting pleasures. Rages, brutality and copulation are rejected as naive. All the libertines are horrified by nature and the natural. They will not tolerate the sight of a plant or herb. Green is reserved for the color of some makeup, some hair, some shirts and stockings. They might even pretend to be ignorant of what a vegetable is.

INFORMATION 5: INTO OBSCURE AND OBTUSE INTERIORITIES

DOCUMENTS: Interview with John Gruen (*Art News*, 1978), Hegel, *Esthetics*, Aubier, 1944,

we do not know whom he wishes to visit. Perhaps in that world visitors jump through the hoops in the same way that circus lions leap through flaming rings. At this point one would remember other strange pictorial hoops, for example, in Lucas Cranach's *La Mélancolie* in which three children are trying to pass through an enormous ring.

Everything would take place as if Planet Lindner, without a trace of nostalgia, had abolished Christian art. There would be no halos around sacred heads. The round halo would be found in the shape of a billiard ball, the wheels of machines and women's breasts.

INFORMATION 3: CORDS

DOCUMENTS: *Boy With Machine* (1954), *The Couple* (1961), *Untitled* (1964), *The Meeting* (1953).

Yes, they would also be interested in strings, twine, threads, ropes, laces and cords. Yes, the children would use them to put together their

Couple. *1977. Oil on canvas. 204 x 178 cm. Galerie Maeght, Paris.*

volume 2, page 163; various paintings.

Information 5 is here undoubtedly to complete the first one on the bestiary of the planet. "Dogs," says Lindner, "like children are the real grown-ups." To be grown-up on Planet Lindner requires the individual not to surrender or become too exteriorized, just to be there, closed in within himself.

We know how Hegel analyzed what he called the degradation of animality. The Hebrews and the Greeks, according to him, degraded what the Hindus and Egyptians revered: "Therefore the animal figure occupies the main place in their artistic representation...before the human being... the human was perceived as the only incarnation of the real. From the moment the spiritual becomes aware of itself, respect for the obscure and obtuse interiority of animal life disappears."

On Planet Lindner everything happens contrary to what occurs in such histories as Georg Wilhelm Friedrich Hegel's. The spiritual would not exist there, crushed between the massive bodies and the space closing in on them. It would not be aware of itself or even of its absence. The concept of truth would have no meaning and it would be hard to understand how it could manifest itself.

Still existing then, insurpassable, definitive — such would be the mark of obscure and obtuse interiorities that make up stubborn children and dogs. On Planet Lindner, moreover, these interiorities are not respected; in fact, the notion of respect does not mean much in this world. Only the vacant stare, the implacable gaze of dogs and children would be noticed and contemplated with a certain fascination and uneasiness.

INFORMATION 6: THE MOHICANS OF THE CAPITALS

DOCUMENT: *The Pipe Smoker* (1976).

He would be called Pipe Smoker and would wear a green shirt, blue tie, mauve suit with yellowish-gray collar and sleeves. He would have a long-haired pigtail knotted with a ribbon. Between his lively red lips he would hold a lighted pipe; and he would watch in silence the rising smoke. His cheek would be marked by a curve whose meaning escapes the spectators, the war paint on a Mohican of the capitals, of a Navajo bearing an urban sprawl. In the bars, boarding houses and hot spots of Planet Lindner, what Bertolt Brecht called the jungle of the cities, the Comanches of the cities would follow their trails. The colors on their skin would indicate the number of their vanquished foes and for them, every painting would be a war painting.

INFORMATION 7: A STRIPPING

DOCUMENT: *Rear Window* (1971); Interview with J. Gruen.

At first glance one would hesitate to compare Planet Duchamp (as it appears in *Grand Verre*, 1915-1923) and Planet Lindner. The comparison might seem to be between only a universe of color and transparency and Lindner's intensity of colors. But this would be wrong. In the first place there would have to be a different conception of color on Planet Lindner, something that went beyond the simple perception; then, color would not be compared merely to Duchamp's blacks, browns and transparencies. Lindner said: "About color, I always felt that to be a good painter one should be color blind because color does not have to be seen; it has to be felt. When I told that to my students they thought I was crazy!"

Curious analogies would arise, those closely related to wheels and gearworks, nudes, uniforms and liveries. Also on Planet Lindner, Brides would live apart from Single Men. Not that men and women would find it difficult and even impossible to communicate with each other. Only that men and women would live according to different colors as if they were breathing another kind of oxygen, as if their senses gave them conflicting data about their surroundings. Perhaps the break between the space for the Brides and that of the Males would be more radical in Lindner's world than in Duchamp's.

Given Duchamp's *Grand Verre*, the Bride would be situated in the upper region and several Male molds would inhabit the lower parts. According to Lindner's *Rear Window*, the Bride would occupy the red world on the left and only one Male would live at the right in a blue space.

The Bride would not be stripped bare by the Males. Already nude, having undressed herself by taking off her corsets, girdles and breast plates, she would have kept on her high heels and dried her body with a towel. A Bride in the bath, an anonymous Suzanne. Perhaps not. Perhaps she would not be a Bride. We could never be sure of it anyway. She might be a ghost or the semblance of a Bride. We might see only her sil-

houette. Perhaps an image of fabric (towel) would be grafted on an image of flesh. As for the male, he would be in uniform but not as a leather-maker, constable, lackey, delivery man, night club bouncer, undertaker, priest, policeman or stationmaster. His uniform would be that of a gangster, as much a prisoner of abstract laws as of the police. If the Bride were only a deceptive shadow, the Male would not be worth more. Under his leather gloves, under his stiff clothing, sometimes made of metal, under his tiger skin coat or one made of steel, he might have neither flesh nor bones; besides, his head might be nothing more than a waxed mask.

Between man and woman on Planet Lindner, it would often be as follows: nothing would happen. Often, yes. Most often, yes. But not always, no...

INFORMATION 8: AN IMMENSE GAMBLING HOUSE

DOCUMENTS: *Ace* (pastel, 1975), *East 69th Street* (1972), *Solitaire* (1973), *The Gambler* (1951), *Untitled* (1962), *The Billiard* (1954-55), *Checkmate* (1966), *Partners* (1971), *L'as de trèfle* (The Ace of Clubs, 1973).

Among other things the planet would be a giant gambling den with chess boards and card games. Many would be cheating. Most of the time they would have the ace (clubs, diamonds) in their hands. Hearts would no doubt be trump. Bald, mustached, with a bare torso, perhaps having already lost his clothing, a player might appear impassive. Some players would have invented cards whose colors might be changed at will. According to one document (*Untitled*, 1962), the same card could be an ace of hearts or an ace of clubs. Two men would be playing billiards from an upside down position and one of them would perhaps be reminiscent of the swindler of *Série Noire*. Others would be betting on the races. Or else, from certain letters and numbers, the painting could evoke the vertical portion of a pinball flipper. At times, what some would see as a target would seem to others like a strange wheel of fortune and misfortune....

Living here would entail facing risk and danger and trying to pervert it by directing it in one's favor. Often this risk would have connections with rectangular surfaces marked with colors — playing cards. Painters are usually interested in games where color and risk operate in two dimensions. Recall, for example, Cézanne's *Card Players* (1893-96); Léger's *Card Party* (1917) which takes place in the trenches, where the risks of war mix with the risks of the game. You might also think of the *Tricheur* (The Cheater, 1615) by Georges de la Tour. Every painting has something to do with card games; it is always a matter of establishing complicities

Leopard Lily. *1966. Oil on canvas. 178 x 152 cm. Rudolf Szwirner collection, Cologne. (Photo Geoffrey Clements.)*

Hello. *1966. Oil on canvas. 178 x 152.5. Harry N. Abrams family collection. New York. (Photo Geoffrey Clements.)*

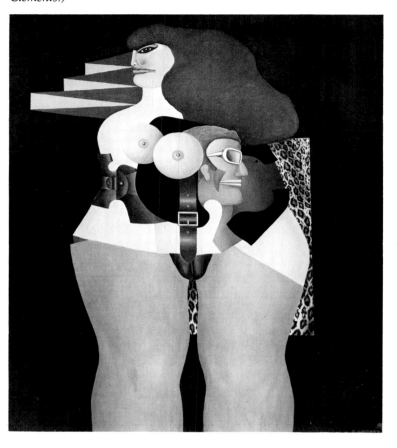

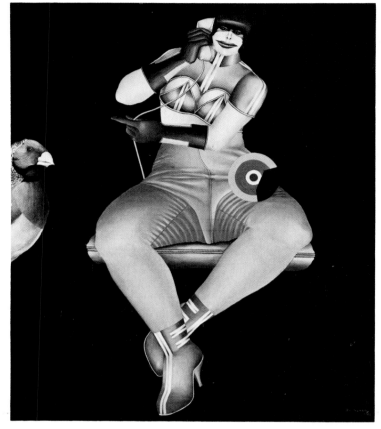

58

with risk to obtain the desired image...

On Planet Lindner many characters would bring to mind the courtly card figures in the deck, and kings and queens would be seen holding aces in their hands.

INFORMATION 9: THE SECRET OF WOMEN

Planet Lindner would seem to the superficial observer a planet without a secret. Fashions would be flashy there. Erotic, aggressive provocations would be discretely avoided. Women would exhibit their breasts, vehemently suggest their sex or make allusions it with their painted lips. By their garters, corsets, boots or pointed shoes, they would seem ready to satisfy every fetish. The men would be gambling their wealth in the offhanded, carefree manner of outlaws and showing off in the style of fashion models.

But it would be a mistake to emphasize only the marvelous affronteries just as it would be a mistake to seek specific secrets beneath appearances. There would not be any veiled secret behind the displays. The startling, brutally indiscrete aspect of each manifestation would already be an inexplicable, mysterious phenomenon. On the other hand, the female inhabitants (and to a lesser degree the males) in their very presence would appear to be the enigmatic beings of Planet Lindner. There would be no possible contact with them; we would simply perceive them as sparkling, sexual enigmas. Lindner evokes the

secret of women in his paintings without being explicit. It is a well-defined secret but not one which would satisfy Freudians or calculators. Lindner only points out the presence of the secret in all its fascinating aspects. "Women," he said, "have more imagination than men. And they have secrets they do not know they possess." Their secret is not one of knowledge; it escapes knowledge. It is more like a force. Some actions are motivated by secrets unknown to the woman who is the source of the secrets. "Nature," the painter said elsewhere, "gives weapons and secrets to the woman at a very early age. From puberty on she has a secret that separates her from males of the same age; but in addition to the secret she has a weapon." The weapon she possesses and uses, however, does not give her pleasure. It seems that having secrets adds to one's sense of power but secrets also, by their fascination and strangeness, cause a certain sadness. There is a definite relationship between secrets and melancholy. "In my paintings of couples," Lindner stated, "it is the woman who is more brilliant, stronger and sadder than her mate." There would certainly be a gap between the perspectives of Lindner and Max Ernst on women. According to Ernst, "the Woman of a Hundred Heads keeps her secret. She guards it." But the women of Planet Lindner would not guard their secrets. Their secrets are there only to protect them and reinforce their sad strength.

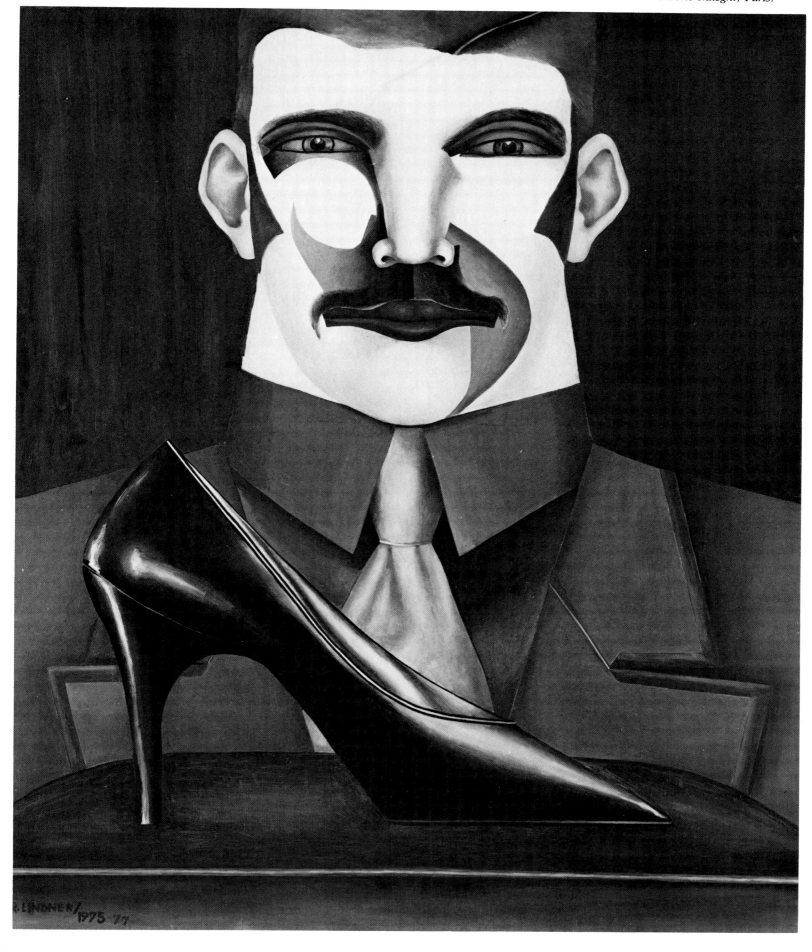

Shoot. *1969. Watercolor.*
60 x 50 cm. Private collection.
(Photo Galerie Claude Bernard,
Paris.)

60

INFORMATION 10: SLOWNESS

Everyone here would move extremely slowly, and every movement would be interrupted by a multitude of poses. The stiffness of clothing would help to slow down gestures. The clothing should not be wrinkled and its creases ought to be respected.

INFORMATION 11: BELOW THE SURFACE

The documents would never show vegetable life; we have to imagine subterranean green-houses and vast mushroom beds that enable the inhabitants to feed themselves.

Several documents would give information about the existence of machines but these would be machines put together by children — mechanical toys. Other machines (those that weave cloth, make corsets, glasses and targets) would be located elsewhere, out of sight, perhaps under the planet's surface. On the surface itself people would be visible, playing games of chance, seducing one another and evading one another's desires. But production (of goods, etc.) would take place elsewhere and would not be visible.

INFORMATION 12: MUSEUM ORGIES

On this planet people would practice what Charles Fourier described in *Le Nouveau Monde Amoureux* as "museum orgies: all the people will reveal in their nudity the beauties deserving of admiration; a woman whose beauty is her bust and throat will expose only her bust; one whose beauty is her rump, the small of her back, her thigh, arm, etc. will expose only that part; and the same goes for men. Each one will display what he/she deems worthy of serving as a model for artists." Many documents from the planet would have as a source the careful painter who observed these museum orgies.

CONTAGION OF THE PLANETS

It is enough that we are informed about the existence of such a planet (literary or pictorial) to understand that gradually its mores and its objects circulate in our environment. In his Preface to *Voyage en Grande Garabagne*, the poet Henri Michaux wrote: "Certain readers have found these countries a bit strange; that will not last. This impression is already passing... These countries, you will note, are perfectly natural and will be found everywhere ...soon." A novella by Jorge Luis Borges *Tlön Uqbar Orbis Tertius* also comes to mind: A group of people invent a planet and describe it in an encyclopedia. Little by little the objects and customs coming from this world called Tlön make their way into our own universe. Gradually, predicted the hero of the novel, "the

Contact. *1977. Oil on canvas. 203 x 138 cm. Private collection. (Photo Galerie Maeght, Paris.)*

61

Englishman, the Frenchman and Spaniard will disappear from the planet. The world will be only Tlön."

Our world perhaps will become more and more "Lindner" with sparkling, sad, secretive women, with machine-like children, stubborn animals, targets, games of chance and a slowing down of everything, everywhere.

GILBERT LASCAULT

the solitary machines
by jean-christophe bailly

Duchamp's *Grand Verre* reveals the story of a secret love with irony and a certain ethereal transparency. The Bride and the bachelors (suitors) are hermetically separated by a double metallic line, a genuine barrier which is not transparent and forces the bachelors to pass over it by resorting to another strategy — firing from a distance so that the sympathy of the "desiring machine" above, always immobile, innocent and ready for anything, is awakened.

After seeing Richard Lindner's *Partners* I was immediately struck by its structural resemblance to Duchamp's great work. The basic components of the Bride are here and are essentially the same but assembled in a reversed arrangement. And although the feminine element is at the bottom and the masculine is at the top they are still brutally separated by a line as in Duchamp's work. The transparent and ironic elements of a secretive distance have been replaced by a certain cruelty devoid of a contrasting background; it is a world depicted in bold colors with no connection plastically to the mercurial ballet of *Grand Verre*. The nine bachelors become one

The Table. *1961. Oil on canvas. 152 x 127 cm. (Photo Galerie Claude Bernard, Paris.)*

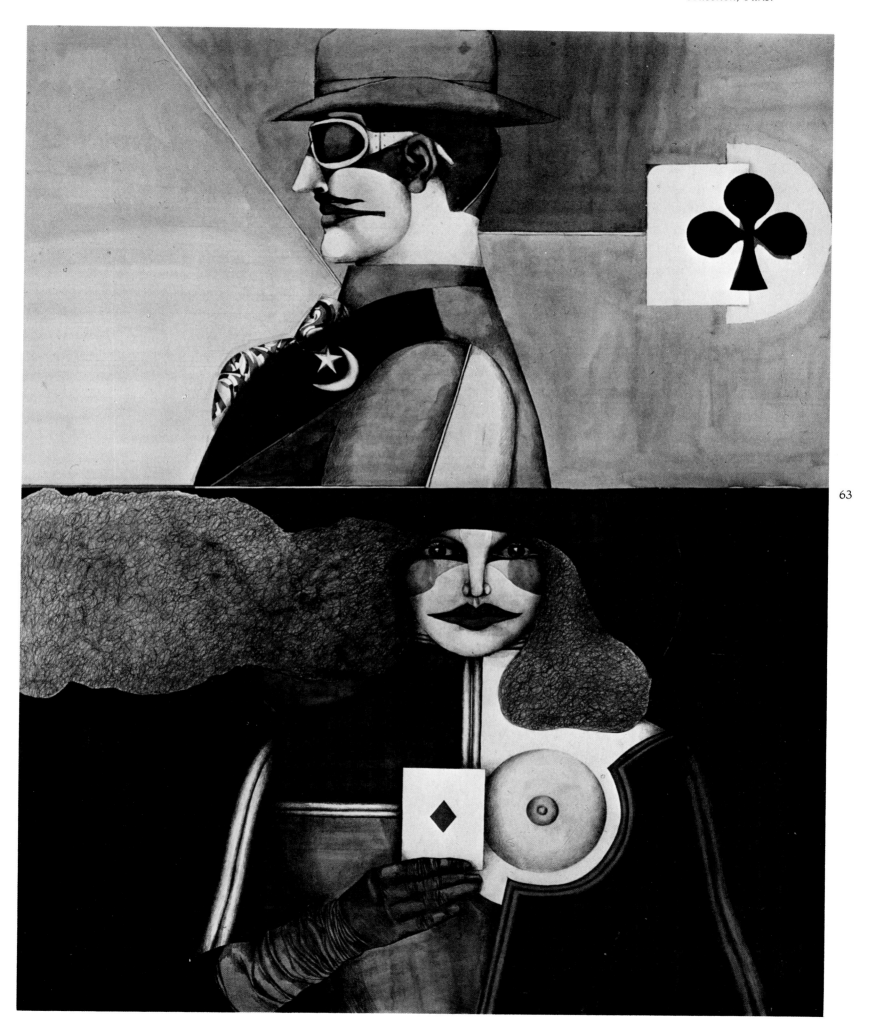

Partners. *1971. Watercolor. 145 x 115 cm. Private collection, Paris.*

63

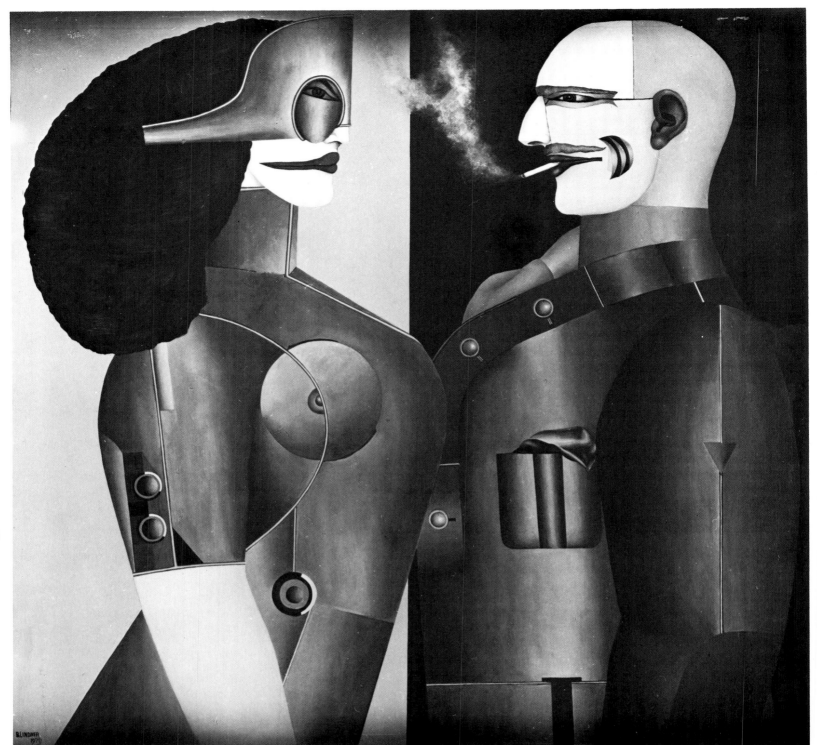

individual while the story of the queen and her suitors becomes that of an ordinary couple: *Partners.* This change from nine to one in which the mythical undergoes a subsequent displacement carries with it a whole panoply: the insects or cordons consisting of "a cemetery of uniforms and liveries" are delineated in an individual (in the upper half of the painting) who is in the garb of a pimp with dark glasses to stress his anonymity. At the bottom is a woman, no longer looking downwards, yet with certain attributes still in tact. Motionless, holding an ace of diamonds in her hands, she appears unagitated, her enigmatic smile and mysterious gesture juxtaposing her hair which seemes to move along like a cloud, like the veil of the Bride. The position emphasizes her ethereal nature but without making her seem too cold-blooded as she steadily fixes her divine-like gaze as if she is dreaming of flight. Her companion remains a human insect without breadth or eyes. Thus the woman's dominant position is maintained and even reinforced by her passage under the dividing line. The fierce Virgin-Bride delivered to the unconscious disorder of her own fragility has given way to a goddess who is clearly placed in a solitary position of dominance; she makes the gesture of offering herself in a way that is both withdrawn and an act of dedication to the tragedy of advertising and anticipation: waiting for, longing for intimacy that would turn the world upside down instead of into the unattractive lethargy of marketable bodies. I find tremendous sadness in this painting, not so much because of the separation but from the total failure that this separation imposes on the

The Couple. 1971. Oil on canvas. 183 x 198 cm. Private collection, New York.

Lithograph of The Window. 1958. Oil on canvas. 127 x 105 cm.

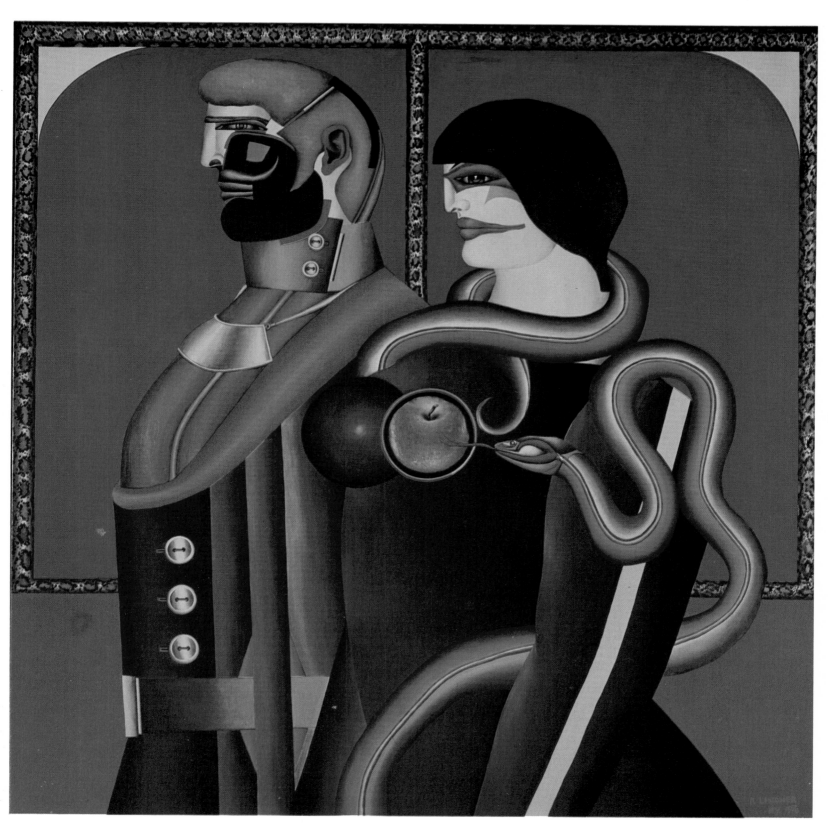

65

And Eve. *1970. Huile sur toile
(Oil on canvas). 183 x 178.5 cm.
Centre National d'Art et de
Culture Georges Pompidou, Musée
National d'Art Moderne, Paris.*

Untitled. *1969. Aquarelle sur papier (Watercolor). 104 x 74 cm. Coll. particulière. (Photo Cordier and Ekstrom, New York.)*

Encounter. *1976. Huile sur toile (Oil on canvas). 180 x 180 cm. Coll. particulière.*

68

The Street. *1963. Huile sur toile (Oil on canvas). 183 x 183 cm. Kunstsammlung Nordrhein-Westfalen, Düsseldorf.*

Couple. *1969. Aquarelle sur papier. (Watercolor). 142 x 117 cm. Coll. Estée Lauder, New York. (Photo Cordier and Ekstrom.)*

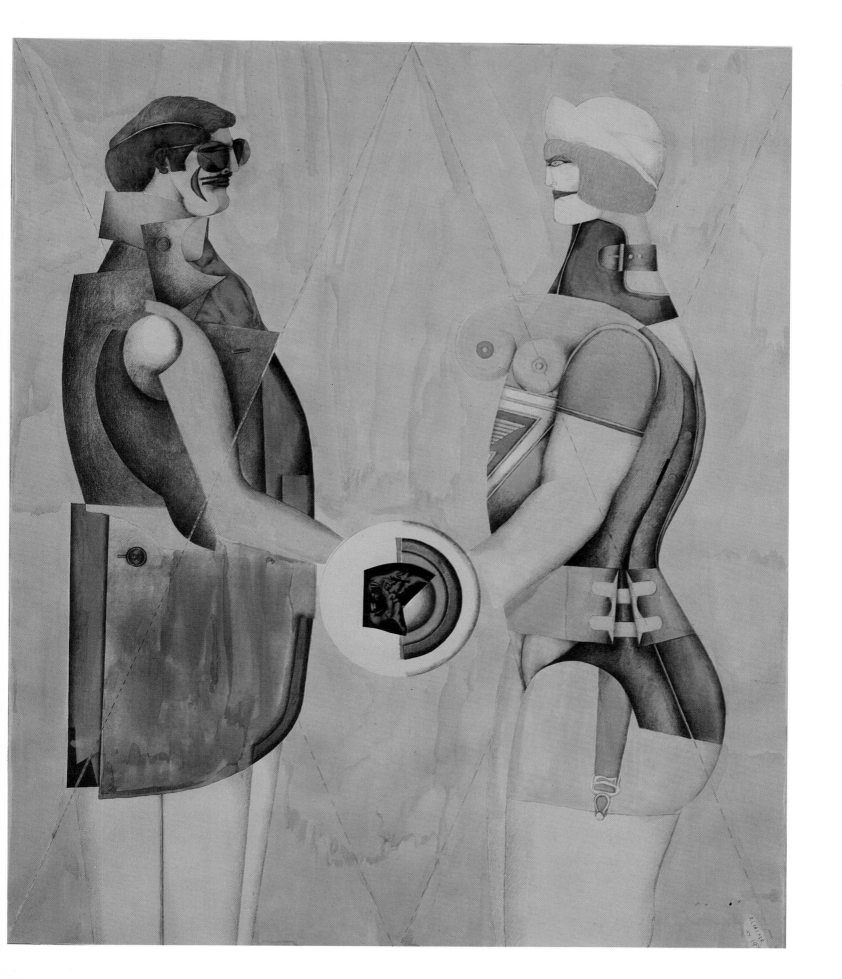

New York City III. *1964. Huile sur toile (Oil on canvas). 178 x 152 cm. (Photo Galerie Claude Bernard, Paris.)*

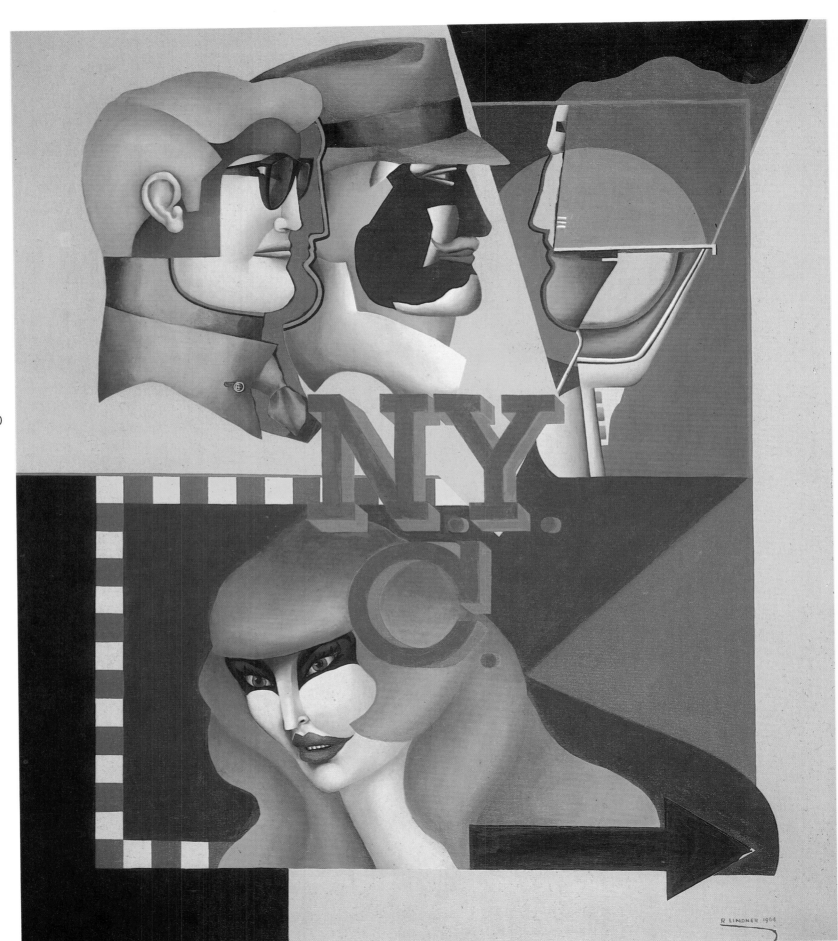

Miss America Indian. *1970. Aquarelle sur papier (Watercolor). 61 x 51 cm. Coll. particulière. (Photo Galerie Maeght, Saint-Paul-de-Vence.)*

73

feminine element. However, the painting has been done by a man; consequently the cross between appearances and vacillations of desire leads to the world that has no love, only the terrible noises of animals that are frightfully alone.

The game really begins with what Apollinaire calls in *Onirocritique* "the different eternities of man and woman," a game in which playing cards are the enduring emblem as they are in Lindner's entire work. Lindner's strength comes from the fact that he has identified the territory of this game as being in the streets. Moreover, he knows how to take this living terrain, impose changes and effect a kind of tragedy akin to popular opera (in the style of early Brecht) where it is impossible to take into account tenderness and cruelty. Under the rules of this game the failure of the lonely creatures who re-

tain their nostalgia for an impossible escape is maintained within the limits of desire for a pleasure that is bursting with color — the world is an aviary.

Boy with Machine, the huge ugly boy who serves from now on as preface to *Anti-Oedipe* and to the fable of the "desiring machines" is roosting. He is alone, at an age when the triumph of onanism gets the upper hand in the dark room. But the true roosting takes place elsewhere; the more or less painful inwardness of adolescence proceeds from the discovery of the world. And the world is modern, animated, and provocative on the other side of the ocean, like a space opening up. New York is where we imagine a little man "with a bird-like profile," eagerly looking at everything in colors that moves and strikes, eagerly looking at the legs crossing the colors. The clumsy and secretive European child remains in reserve in the little man's head, but it is the world — men and women passing without being seen — the infinite world of already imaginary beings of the city that is from now on identified as a machine and as a game. The automatic insertion of mythology into the space creates the charm in which the players pass. Transfigured, they become brilliant. Multiple figures of a fixed game from which only the dogs escape, they weave the chromatic skein of the routes whose streets spread their secret into infinity.

The Street (1963) first appeared as the exact New York equivalent of *La Rue* by Balthus, but the balance between the sacred and the anecdote which is the strength of the painting by the French artist is disrupted in the one by Lindner. The replacement of the anecdote by a play of interrupted zigzag planes introduces a violence in which each seems to be commanded to be his or her own person. The harmony of the religious "bath" in which Balthus placed his characters gives way to a tense, yet motionless world that produces no communication. The fanaticism of being oneself finds expression only in the bold honesty of object-bodies that are completely isolated from each other. This painting, echoing *The Meeting*, which is ten years older, is like a parade of characters who either alone or two by two are going all the way to embody the possibilities set down in the rules of Richard Lindner's game.

The rule: Separation.
The game: Meeting
(And vice-versa).

The first example (since *Partners*, more than an example is the emblematic summary of Lindner's urban poem): *Moon over Alabama.* A man and a woman pass each other in a space, namely the street. The woman in the foreground conceals half of the man. They seem to be one within the other and yet separating, like an androgynous being caught at the moment when it is splitting into its two parts; the glances — the woman's whorish and conquering and the man's limited and nearly invisible — already fixed in opposite directions are fiercely opposed. They are going to meet with a fate that has no mystery, but this absence of mystery is the enigma of colored, vulgar, hieratic insects. The non-mystery and non-melancholy of a street, and yet the silence exists, and yet the painting takes the shape of this silence.

Second example: *Rear Window.* The man and the woman are both posed as archetypes and face each other in the perfect and most complete of minimal panoplies — all the accessories are reduced to a mustache-necktie combination for the man and to a made-up painted eye-breast combination for the woman. Motionless, they

Richard Lindner's studio.
(Photo Piotr Trawinski.)

could, they ought to see each other. But they are shut up within themselves in the silent unreality of platitude, the woman perhaps giving a ghost of a smile beyond the painting — a smile that by definition rejects all attachments. The horizontal line of *Partners* this time separates their profiles vertically, prohibiting every attempt at escape from the game's limits[1]. The very reality of appearance riveted to an illusory presence yields nothing, looks out on nothing; the window is a wall. But perhaps the world is not like this. What makes *Encounter* the most beautiful and most unforgettable of Richard Lindner's paintings is that the dividing line is invisible there and

74

Rear Window. *1976. Gouache.*
(Photo Piotr Trawinski.)

Rear Window. *1976. Oil on canvas. 200 x 170 cm. Galerie Maeght, Paris.*

119th Division. *1963. Oil on canvas. 203 x 127 cm. Walker Art Center. (Photo Geoffrey Clements.)*

76

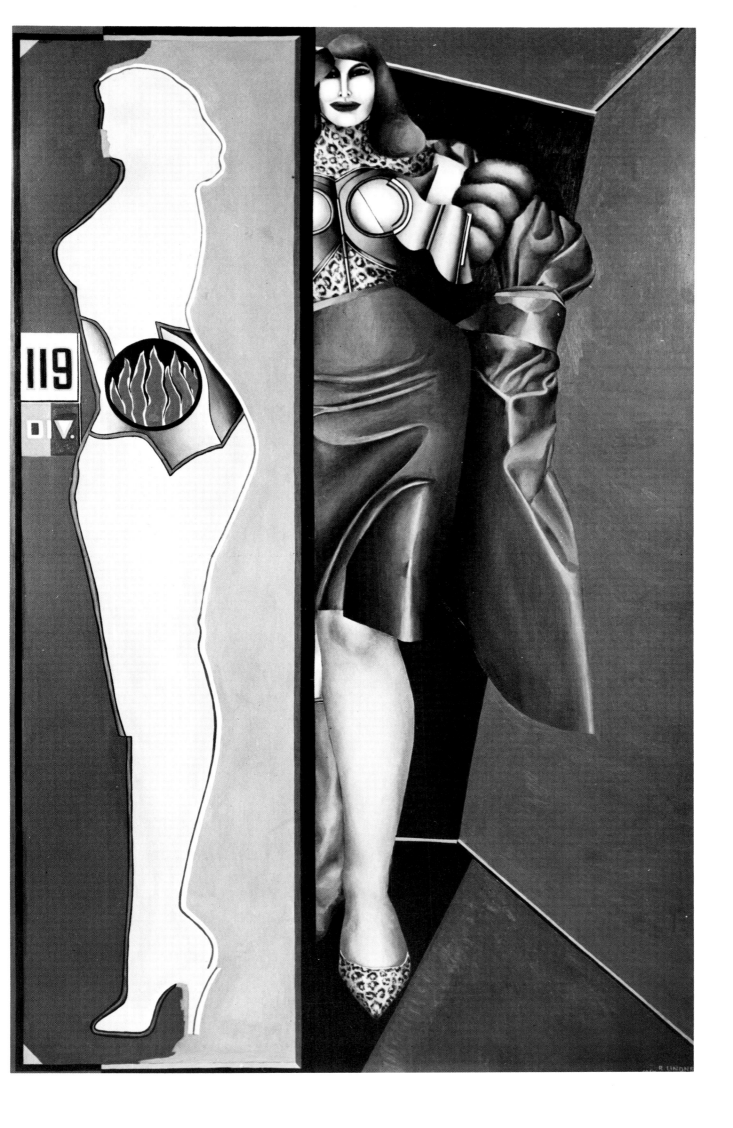

the space carved out by the absent line gives consistency to the sense of madness that is lacking in the painting of the window. This is not a criticism but a transition. From *Partners* and all the other paintings presenting separation in a deliberate way, I had to arrive at this one in which the separation is figurative in the title and the very appearance of the meeting.

In profile, a horseman is dressed like a man and made up with a shadow the size of a loupe around the eyes; the woman with her bust and hairdo solidly occupies the foreground of the painting; in the background, facing the other way, the man seems this time less of a pimp than a dandy or a cavalier. Like her, he is silent and intent. They don't see each other or the dog who, between them, becomes part of the oblique line as he too imposes his silence and canine gaze on them. Above them is the moon, which may in fact be the sun, but everything is detached from the dark background and in separated planes is isolated and fixed in an indefinite suspension.

If one thinks about immobility and the glances of Carpaccio's *Courtisanes* one sees that the petrified daydream no longer depends on anything since there are no objects in this painting. There are only three gazes, like indifferent vectors, and the void between them. One thinks that in this emptiness there is a sacred weight, a suspended terror, or a latent crime. But everything remains within, congealed in the compelling power of an image that resists identification and eludes words. One understands at last that fantasms, love, terror, tenderness and an astonishing acuity have come to rest far from all ethics at the feet of the voyeur who comes apart there as in a dream, a consuming dream that ended by forcing the artist to paint and to attain through the image the realm in which women are always stealing away — passing figures offering to a being desiring to possess of which the painting remains the best and the most enduring representation.

Richard Lindner's strength in having transposed this representation of the world to the street, having transposed the oldest myths into the colorful festival of New York, planting the sword separating Tristan and Isolde in the sands of Coney Island, two steps from the booths and the fast-food places, as if the eternal return of "different eternities" had only the change of scenery for amusement.

JEAN-CHRISTOPHE BAILLY

Telephone. *1966. Oil on canvas.*
178 x 152.5 cm. Kuntshalle
Nürenberg, Sammlung Inter-
nationaler, Zeitgerrössicher.
Nüremberg.

(1) In *And Eve* this line also returns, ironically decorated, but this time separating a couple walking together. Thus all the appearances of the couple — the absence of motion, the going in different and in the same directions (a strange walk to tell the truth) — are found facing that opaque screen.

the carnival of memory
by jean-dominique rey

In looking at early photographs of cities it is astonishing to see empty streets, deserted avenues and barren plazas as if crowds had vanished into thin air in the aftermath of some kind of mysterious disaster. Call it man's rebellion against the lens.

The phenomenon is explained by the length of time needed for an exposure — about twenty minutes — as well as by the insensitivity of the plates. Only a portion of reality, the fixed elements such as stones, metals and monuments, could be transmitted while clouds, running water, trees stirring in the breeze or passers-by failed to make an impression and became blurry, undefinable shadows and apparitions. In other words, mobility as it applies to all aspects of real life could not be transmitted. The print showed only the setting, the frame, the scene in which the action was unfolding.

Richard Lindner's painting a century later depends on the opposite phenomenon. The action unfolds within a city which is at best indicated by a few references here and there or by several types of surfaces — sombre flat planes, symbolic angles, fragments of placards or some vague geographical reference. The city (or setting) is never actually shown, nor is it even perceived. Central to the canvas is the character. Faces and bodies command the viewer's attention because of their conspicuousness and have the appearance of a colossus ready to spill over the frame, invade the space and consume it with their inexorable presence.

Thus we find ourselves confronted with a paradox within a painter who is the least acquainted with nature. There is never the slightest trace of the countryside, of a flower, a tree or a river in the artist's work. The citified artist who could not live anywhere but within the confines of a city never represents the city itself; the city exists, but strictly by the relationship that connects it with the strange fauna who inhabit it or who live on the painter's canvas.

When we examine the reasons for the city's absence-presence, they provide one of the keys to this oeuvre. If all Richard Lindner's painting is born of the shock of New York, the city was, as a matter of fact, only a vehicle — the opportunity to make a whole world buried in the artist's memory reappear, a world till then repressed by the dramatic circumstances of life, circumstances that kept him from becoming a full-time painter until he was in his fifties. He never stopped carrying this world, from the time of his childhood, through his exiles, embellishing it and developing it through the years as his fortunes changed.

When at last this world comes into view on the canvas, glittering freely without restraints, it appears as a theatre of memory, a descent into the primordial depths, a kind of *urtragödie* to which New York lends its harsh colors, its neons, all its signs of modernity. But this world will remain for the most part a world of first impressions, early traumas, incipient terrors, initial surprises, and it will retain these peculiar dimensions of childhood, this exaggerated relationship that exists between the child's view of the world and the adult's, namely a suspended perception.

At this level it is symptomatic that one of Lindner's early canvases, circa 1950, was an attempt at a portrait of Marcel Proust, a somewhat clumsy but moving painting, and in any case, a true confessionary work. Marcel Proust, with his shadowy look, is the Lar who at birth presides over the search for things past that had been undertaken by Lindner, or to be more accurate, over the reconquest of the past for which the shrillness of New York gave the starting signal.

From then on New York becomes the background against which memories awaken and blossom, become expressed and transformed; New York is the tumultuous springboard that pulls memories out of the past. The city is a symbol, an analogical grid. All the seething obsessions of childhood with all the terrifying seductive, attractive and fascinating characters that so impressed Lindner during his early years are silhouetted behind boldly made-up faces, flashy garments, amazons of artifice, bedizened grooms, plotting nymphets, gigolo gangsters and deadly mothers.

Most of the figures who are anchored so vividly and with so much horror and anguish on the canvas are stiffly embedded in their roles; with an imperturbable seriousness and unrelenting reality they lie somewhere between the robot and the marionette. They spring out of Lindner's visions of childhood which was in Nuremberg, the city *par excellence* of toys and of famous shops and stores. Throughout his life Lindner perpetuated Nuremberg's captivating presence by collecting toys which he then lost in each successive exile; later, at each new stage of his life he began again with inexhaustible patience to collect them as if he were trying to preserve an important creative source.

But his figures are also born from an expressionism that the artist learned from the theater and cinema in the years preceding Nazi power. This experience helped create the gamut of artificial creatures, mechanical and strange golems, wax mannequins, monstrous and deadly puppets and robots that seem ready to seize control of the artist's world without warning.

The New York of the fifties, with its fascinating crowd life, its keen taste for Kitsch, its resolutely artificial characters, its mechanical exaggeration, revitalizes this dual vision that permeated Lindner every day from his birth to the age of thirty, makes it reappear and rebound

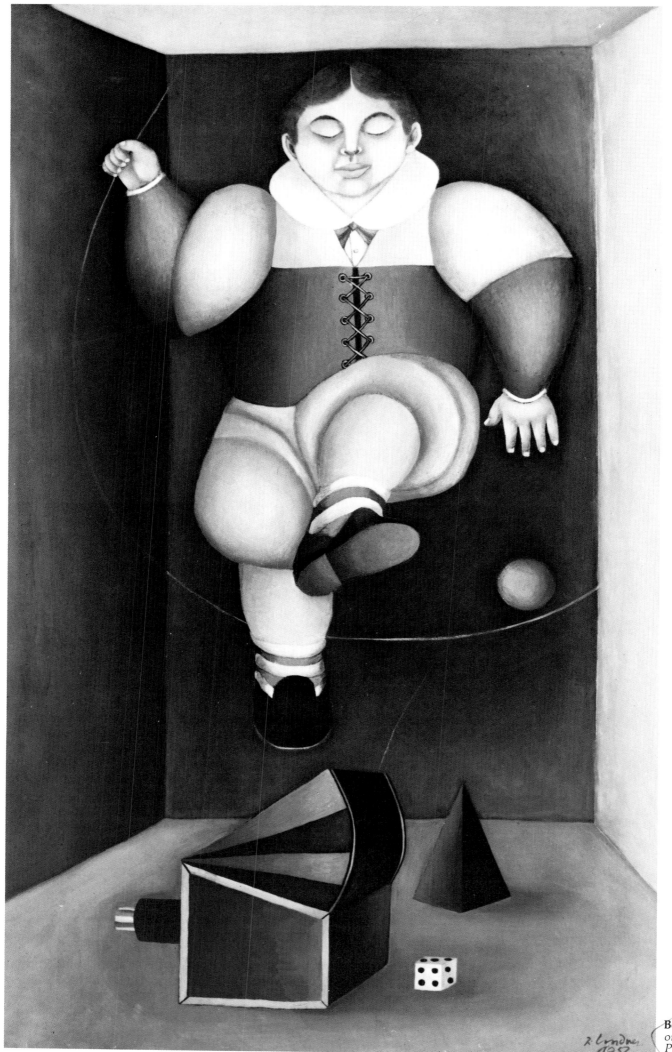

The Child's Dream. *1952. Oil on canvas. 126.5 x 76 cm. Mr. and Mrs. Theodore V. Marsters collection, Whitney Museum of American Art, New York. (Photo Geoffrey Clements.)*

Boy with Machine. *1954. Oil on canvas. 101.5 x 76 cm. Private collection.*

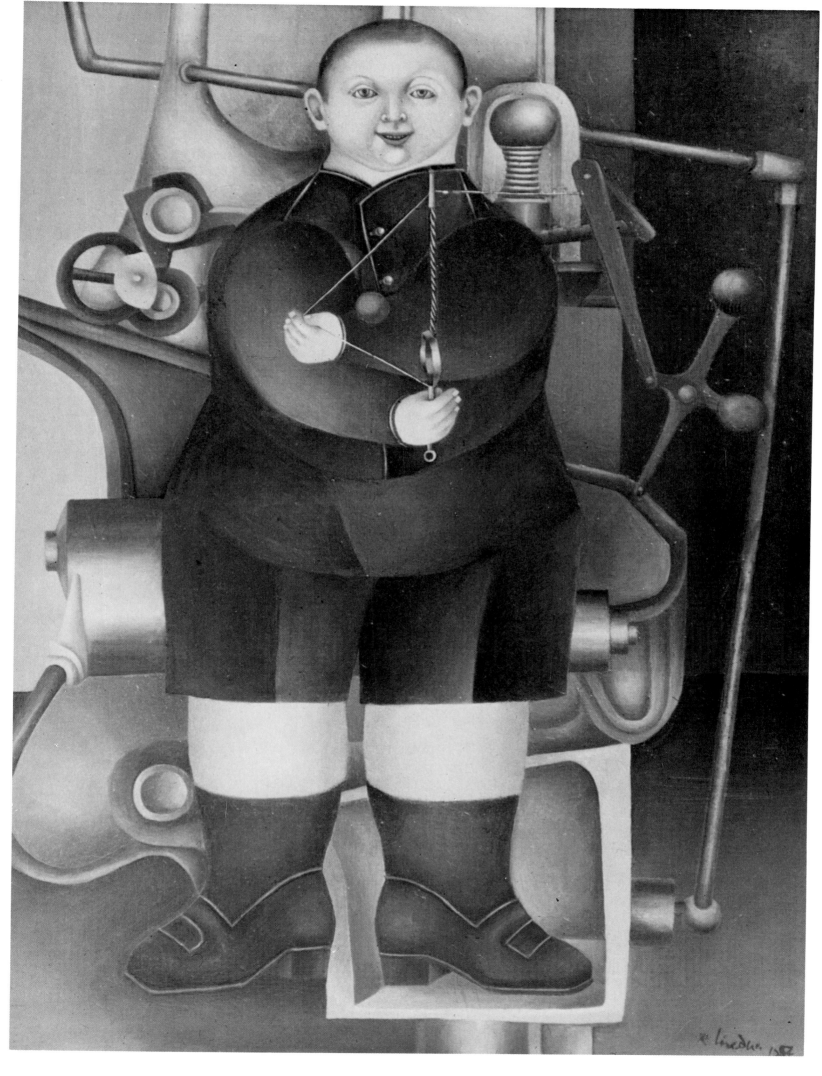

like a real carnival of memory and offers Lindner a tangible version, a projection by turns nightmarish and ludicrous. With his monumental poster sense, his citified taste for the setting, with his visual acuity, which is always on the lookout for a ridiculous and sublime spectacle, the painter gives the vision of a new dimension: the memorialist becomes a visionary witness. Because suddenly the past and the present come together, because the everyday rediscovers the disproportion of memory that is dreamed and amplified by distance, the work finally emerges from its ore and explodes.

Lindner created a world in which the dream and the obsession, the history and the reality, the far and the near, childhood and life to come, imagination and humor, the animal and the mechanical, guile and nostalgia merge or come face to face, telescope each other or collide, mingle or perhaps ignore each other. It is a world that is always enclosed by the night or by the walls of a windowless room, irremedially enclosed, a world of harsh snapshots that is suddenly fixed, a world in which our era is summarized rapidly and reads like an open book, and from which strong colors reflect the sound and the fury in increasing echoes.

But perhaps, as in memories or in dreams, it is a world in which people have lost their shadows. There are distinct blacks, sections of red walls, purplish curtains, garish yellow beaches, green sheets and blue screens. Yet none of the actors in this tragi-comedy ever projects a shadow on the ground. The shadow is absorbed or killed by the harshness of the colors as if the neons of the megalopolis annihilated human existence or as if exile and its obstacles had stripped it of this dimension.

We could speak endlessly about such paintings. But in addition there is another domain to Lindner's work that is less well-known and until now less understood but which nevertheless meant a great deal to the artist. The canvas, that painful and final operation on which Lindner labored for months — in the twenty-seven years from 1950 until his death he completed only 103

Woman. 1970. Oil on canvas.
190.5 x 140 cm. Private
collection. (Photo Geoffrey
Clements.)

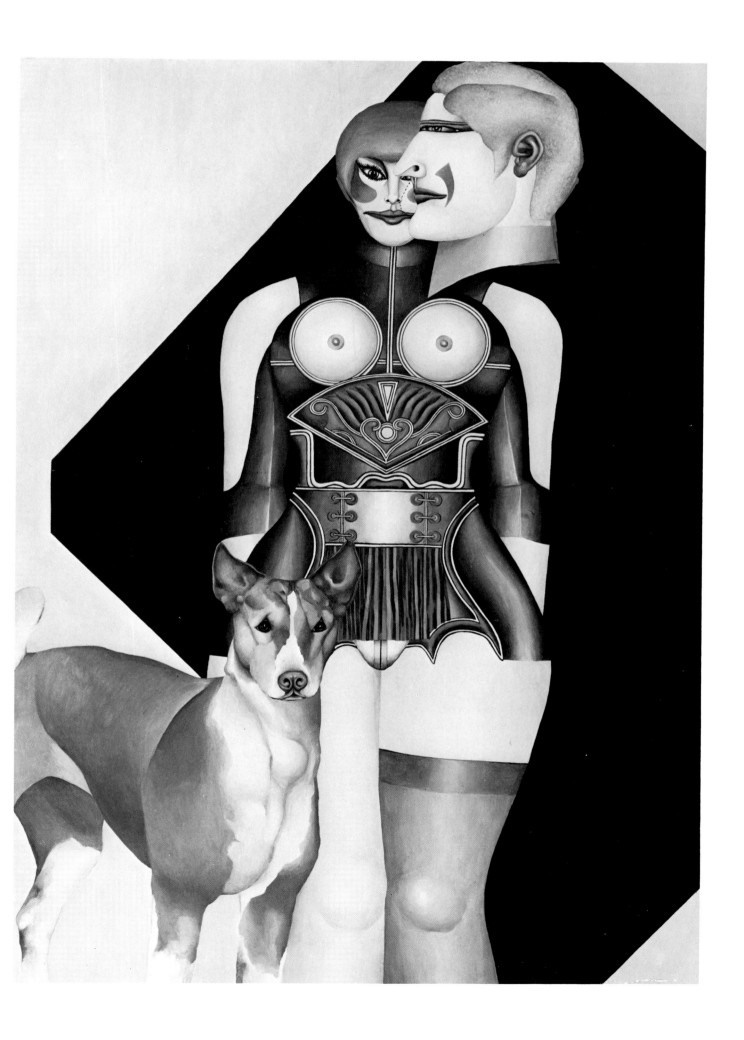

The Pipe Smoker. *1976. Oil on canvas, 100 x 200 cm. Galerie Maeght, Paris.*

paintings — and each time the canvas was preceded by a series of drawings in which every element of composition was established, laid out and then given its place in the whole scheme.

For each of his canvases there exists a kind of dossier, a veritable "preliminary oeuvre," a subterranean "work in progress," thanks to which the Lindnerian process can be scrutinized.

In these drawings the harsh colors disappear or rather do not yet exist; color is still in limbo. Shadow and light are conveyed by lines and occasionally by volume, and sharpness is expressed by concentration on the motif gathered together like a tiger ready to spring or like one plane being projected onto another. The artist is more at ease in these drawings, seeming to prefer the flash, the spark as opposed to the final execution — in short, the invention to the completion.

In examining these sequences, the work resembles an animated film in the course of which we pass from the simple sketch to the final squaring up which is the last stage in the sequence of drawings. Lindner first enriched his initial plan by scrutinizing the details and incorporating them, then made the image more complex by simplifying the features, and finally, with a confident hand drew a definitive character. Each of these drawings is like a movement that comes to take its place in the final symphony. Lindner's graphic work, contrary to that of many artists, proceeds more frequently by additions than by subtractions.

In looking at these dossiers chronologically — inasmuch as some drawings are dated in rela-

tion to the completed painting — what is striking is that once again they begin with a series of children — unusual children, conceived of like dolls sunken in chairs with their eyes glued to the ceiling or else standing on platforms holding sextants in their hands with their heads touching the ceiling as if the world is encircling them and they are trying to push back its limits — children that are both playing with toys and behaving like them at the same time, the actors and the acted upon so that their role becomes a function. Or, as in the first drawing, they stand up against a profile of machinery whose wheels, levers, pulleys, transmission cables, etc. appear in the second act like pieces of a puzzle that suddenly invade the play; by the final act the machinery has changed the child into a machinist who moves about like a programmed system or mechanized robot.

The fact is that in the beginning of the last series the child has a face; in the following drawing the face is only outlined; and in the final drawing the face is a circle without any attempt to draw in features. These characteristics will reappear in the painting where the child is drawn without any human expression — just a monstrous statue swallowed up in a mechanical function.

This child will soon turn into a woman who will appear as an absolutely mechanical creature, a cog. Her predatory presence, her encroaching and dominating fullness makes her into a terrible divinity, something of a glutton, ferocious yet entirely artificial. Her nudity is only glimpsed at; her body is armed with com-

Circus-Circus. *1973. Oil on canvas. 203 x 178 cm. Private collection.*

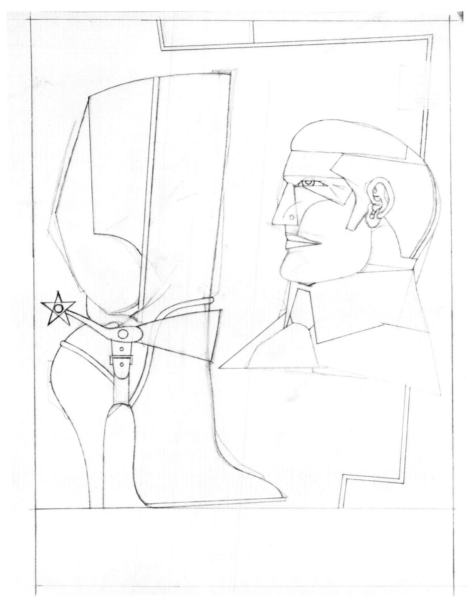

Man's Head. *1973. Pencil drawing. 63 x 50 cm. Private collection. (Photo Piotr Trawinski).*

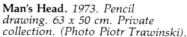

Military Parade. *1950. Pencil drawing. 27.5 x 23 cm. Private collection.*

plicated corsets, iron clothing, a real metallic prosthesis that is both aggressive and defensive-looking and accentuates her fascinating inaccessibility.

Once again the drawings reveal the different stages. Lindner constructed the drawings as an engineer. He took several fragments and studied their form in successive sketches, then in more and more detail until all were finally assembled like pieces of a vast puzzle which the memory guided from the initial to the final image.

However, he also constructs his drawings as he would build a mechanical doll. If a woman happens to be the object, she is not a woman in the usual sense but only to the extent that an image — poster, statue or photo — remains a con-

crete object, above all, to the extent that an obsession becomes an object of feeling or fascination.

In touching upon the essence of America which is a prematriarchal and automated civilization we discover the dominant voyeuristic element that pervades Lindner's art. In this respect he is still one of the outstanding witnesses of his time. For a long time the child had been socially segregated and hence condemned to being a voyeur as far as the mysteries of life, love and women are concerned. Today this voyeurism has spread to all of society and is orchestrated by society's structure, its methods and its goals: from advertising to the televised image, from the magazine to the poster, repetitious images and

Ludwig II. *1974. Black pencil. 18.6 x 18 cm. Private collection. (Photo Piotr Trawinski.)*

88

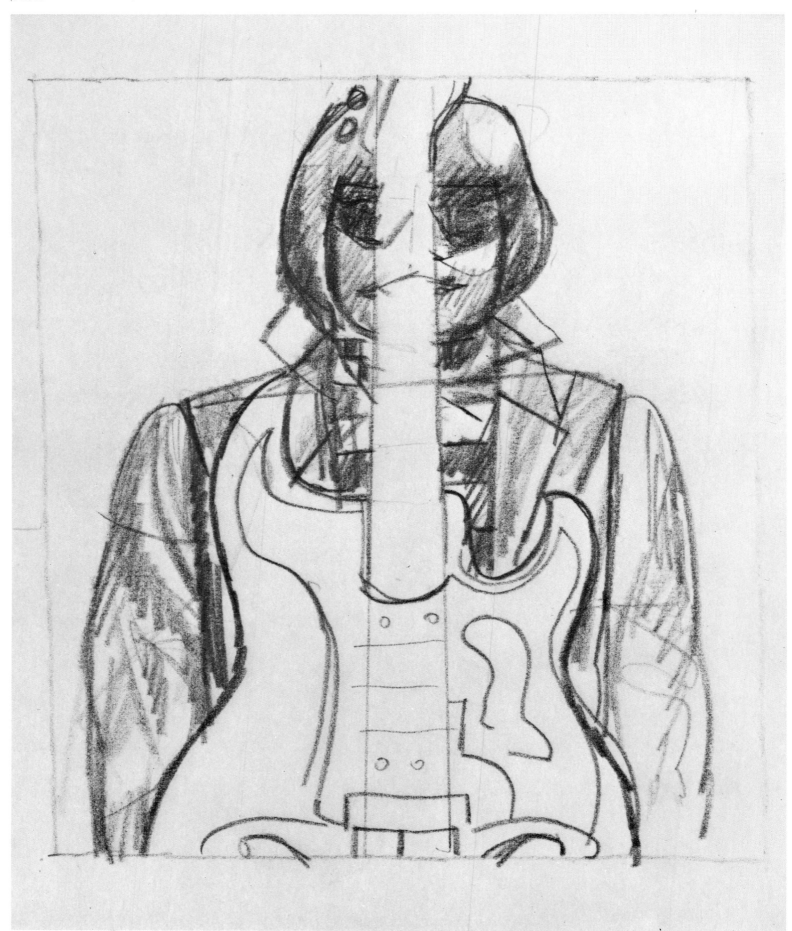

The Chase. *1976. Huile sur toile (Oil on canvas). 204 x 153 cm. Galerie Maeght, Paris.*

90

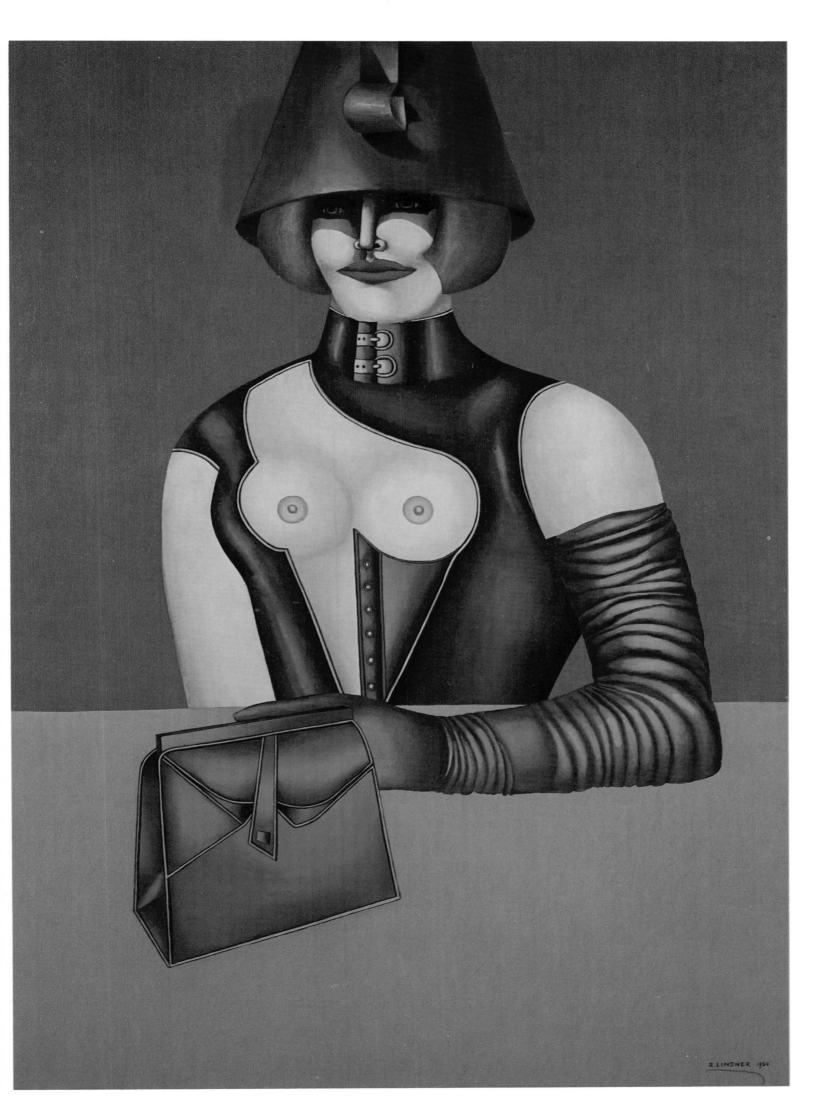

Girl with Green Hair. *1972. Huile sur toile (Oil on canvas). 228.5 x 165 cm. Fischer Fine Art Ltd., London. Knoedler Inc., New York.*

The Target. *1959. Huile sur toile (Oil on canvas). 152 x 102 cm. (Photo Galerie Claude Bernard.)*

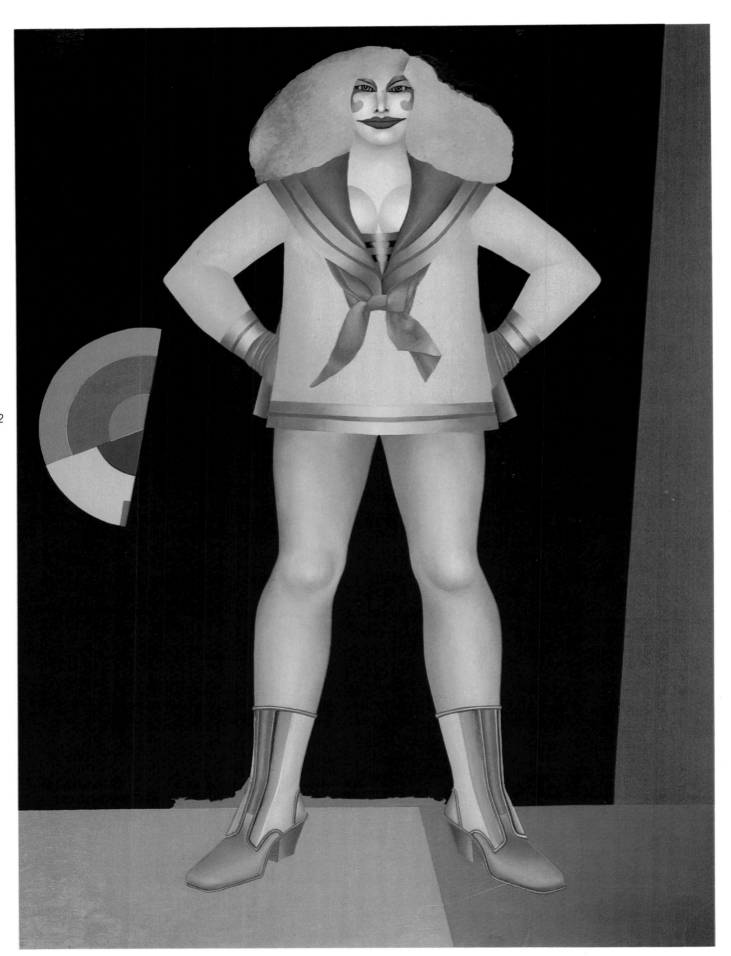

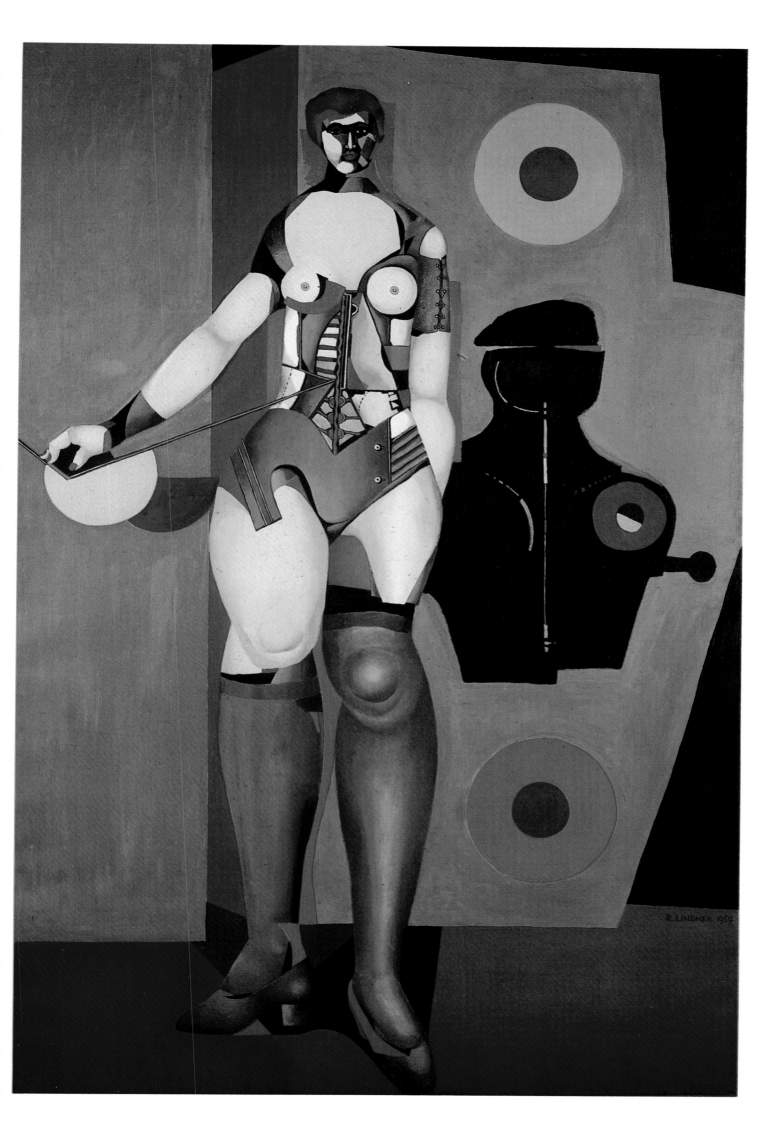

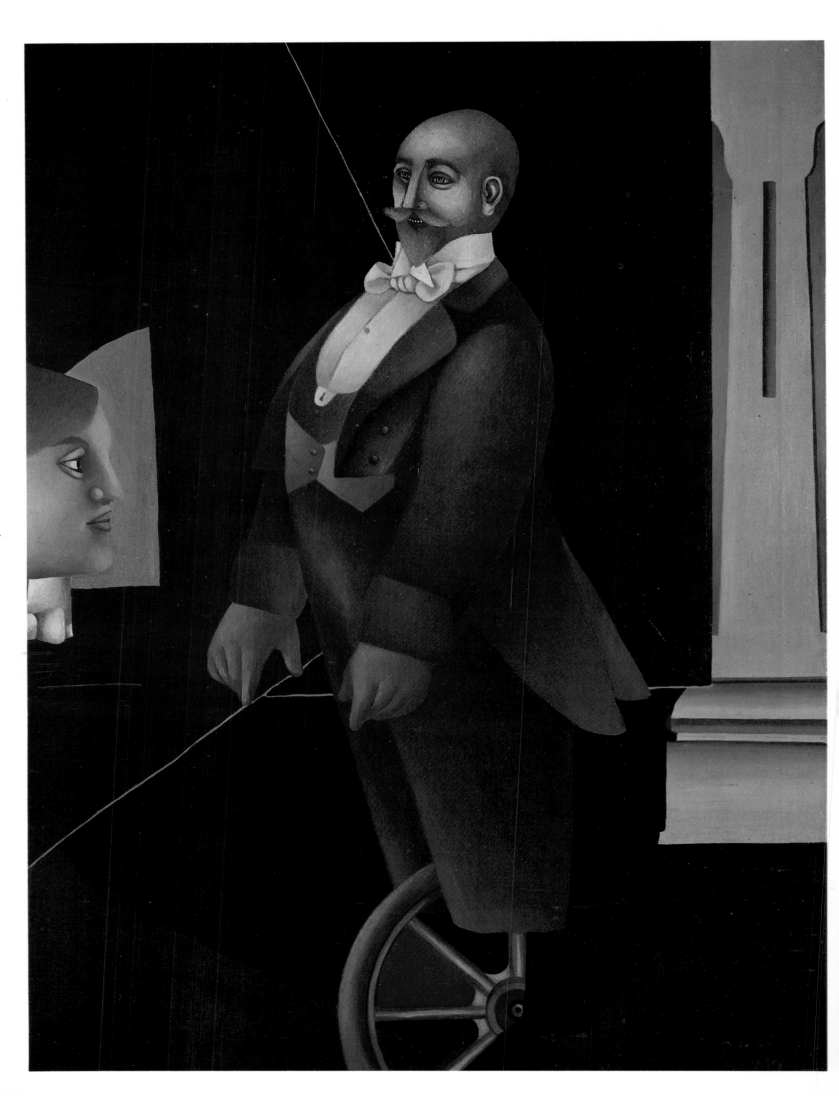

The Wheel. *1954. Huile sur toile (Oil on canvas). 115 x 90 cm. (Galerie Maeght, Paris.)*

Academician. *1954. Pastel, huile et encre sur papier (Pastel, oil and ink). 71.5 x 56 cm. Coll. Richard Lehfeldt, New York.*

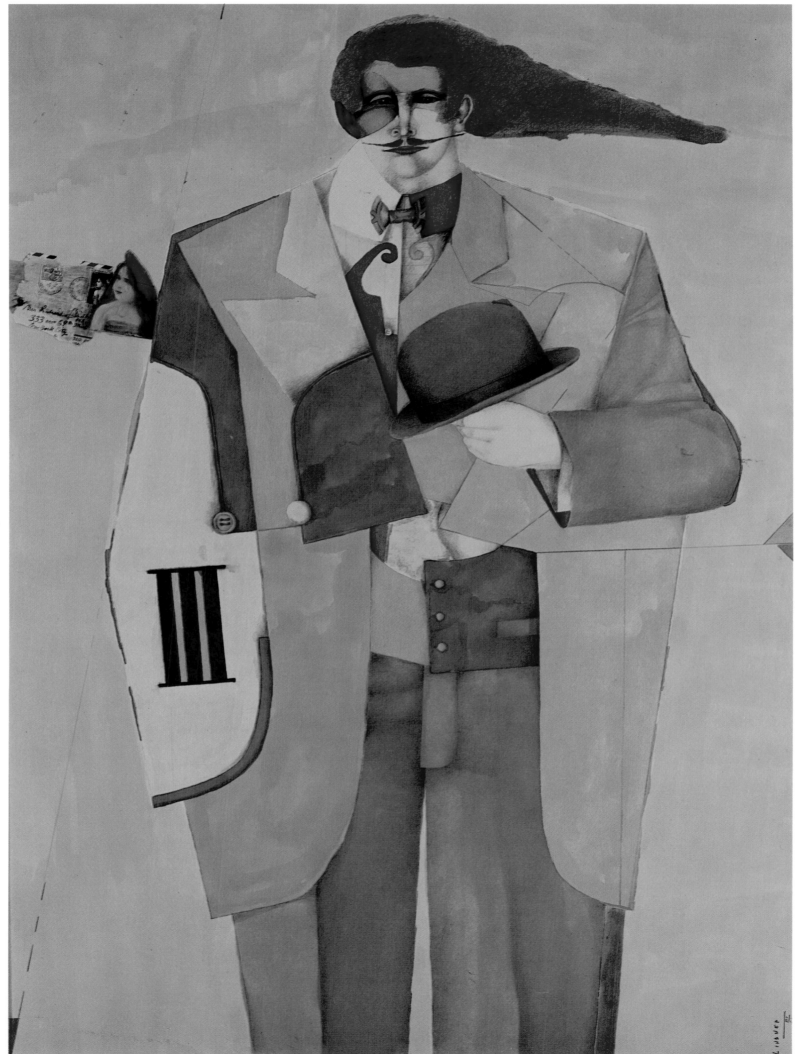

98

all media reinforce the stance. The urban man is a permanent voyeur, condemned by the image to the passivity of the gaze.

From *The Meeting* (1953) which is preceded by an elaborate drawing, the child (in the upper area), the man-king (Ludwig II of Bavaria) and the spectator (on the right) seated on a chair are all reduced to the status of motionless voyeurs while the woman is shown in different states and plays the role of actress towards whom all eyes are turned. This same scenario is found in most of Lindner's drawings and paintings: the man is reduced to looking at or following the woman. Most often only the profile of the man is visible while the woman is full face. Sometimes, as in *Couple*, they face each other but the original drawings disclose a separate geometrical arrangement with a large triangle that seems to move them apart and a central sphere that conceals their hands. Elsewhere they will be placed in two separate areas as two busts on different tiers of a shop window. In *Woman* (1970) the man is nothing more than a superimposed head.

From voyeurism to fetishism is only a matter of degrees and the drawings even better than the paintings reveal to us the passage from one to the other according to an ineluctable process in which the voyeur undergoes a progressive reduction and the object of his fascination becomes enlarged. In the first drawing a very broad man, viewed from the front, seems to be surrounded by two women's shoes of normal proportions. In the next drawing a shoe occupies the foreground and the man fixes his gaze on it. Later, the shoe becomes a boot enlarged to the dimensions of a sheet and the man has disappeared. When he reappears he will be reduced to the profile of just his head, considerably smaller than the shoe he is still staring at.

But beyond the shoes of these actresses, the provocative corsets and suggestive handbags, the fetishist's arsenal, exceeding its customary limits, spreads to all objects of city life as well as to the signals that color and certain geometries transform into targets, the fetish symbols both of the city and of the voyeur's gaze, the trapper and the trapped.

All of Lindner's work develops in this way, within a vast labyrinth that is coded, invisible and permanent. There seems to be neither a clear perspective nor an escape. No oeuvre adheres more closely to its time than does Lindner's, opening onto man's loneliness, his pointless efforts to pierce through what cannot be communicated, his quest for a transcendence that has vanished of which his fantasies are only the muted reflections; his oeuvre is a mirror that constantly causes man to withdraw within himself and to the city which protects him and gives him a sophisticated nature at the same time that it becomes a shell that imprisons him and from which there is no escape except through intermittent outbursts of humor.

JEAN-DOMINIQUE REY

lindner's great game
by alain jouffroy

good artile

Before writing about a painter, one ought to have a certain understanding of the artist's intentions, or perhaps share similar real-life experiences. This would give a certain solid foundation for discussing the artist's work. But such a foundation is often lacking among those who are habitually more concerned with composing a fine text or showing off their own ideas than with understanding the artist's work.

I don't think, however, that anyone should stifle his desire to write about an artist since the article should not be regarded as a definitive interpretation or as a cultural guide for tourists. Rather, the author should undertake the project with the idea of discovering the limits of his own perceptions after which he should become more objective. More often than not, there will be a gap between the article that discusses the painting and the painting itself. There are also paintings that cannot be reconciled with any written word, and others that lend themselves so well to commentary and analysis that they are destined to become conversation pieces.

I wondered, right from the start, whether Lindner's work lends itself to any sort of literary, psychoanalytical or socio-political interpretation, and decided that it did. His characters inspire reverie; their obvious identities as whores, pimps, cops, gangsters, young girls, circus riders, gamblers, etc. seem to encourage a kind of free and romantic-poetic commentary. A Marxist or psychoanalytical interpretation would only make Lindner's work more inscrutable. Wade Stevenson conveyed the extent of the difficulties in his phrase, "Richard Lindner's secrets." I'm not sure I was able to overcome any of the problems he encountered.

Richard Lindner reminds us of another European painter, Saul Steinberg. The two were friends and found fulfillment, but not because they happened to have emigrated to the United States. Hidden, ambiguous relationships link their seemingly unrelated works. Some critics have tried to reduce Steinberg's genius to drawing and caricature. Yet his paintings are so graphic in the freedom of line, composition and ideas that emerge that it is ridiculous to call his work mere cartoons. Lindner's genius, which seems at first glance so pictorial, is really more closely related to drawing, to the vision of a great draftsman, or the sketches of a dreamer. The proper question is: where does Steinberg's painting begin and Lindner's drawing end. It is important to try and discover the subtle seriousness behind Steinberg's work, as well as the secretive if not difficult-to-grasp humor behind Lindner's. The key or principal secret to both artists lies in their desire to be non-obvious and non-trivial to the viewer; understanding their secret, which is not necessarily the same secret, means understanding what is not apparent.

Girl. *1958. Watercolor and lead pencil. 64.5 x 42 cm. Max and Lynda Palevsky collection, Los Angeles.*

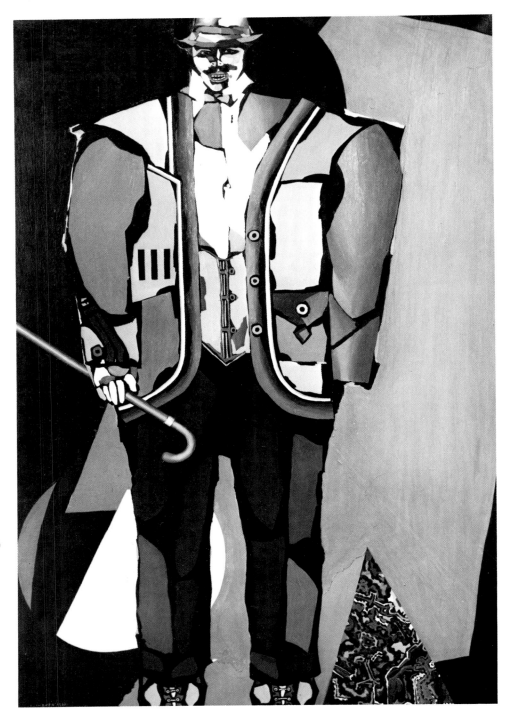

Coney Island. *1961. Oil on canvas.*
60 x 40 cm. Noah Goldowsky Gallery.
(Photo Geoffrey Clements.)

of Pop art has never been clearly analyzed. I believe that his work *Fillette*, in 1955, offers a solution, with the deliberately flattened figures that disguise the real drama. Lindner hides reality behind the display of shop windows where objects are enlarged or reduced in order to shield his vulnerable, subjective vision that is a product of his social history.

If humor is defined in Freudian terms, namely the revenge of the pleasure principle on the reality principle, then everything that contributes to this revenge, beginning with the joy of playing or of imitating others in order to exorcise them, should be considered a form of liberation through humor. Lindner's early paintings are dark and heavy; something is slowly unfolding in them, analogous to the moments in a film before a crime is committed. The characters appear awkward and stiff, withdrawn, taciturn while their clothing is scrupulously adapted to reinforce the sense of mystery; moreover, the stage is filled with doors and walls. This is the very atmosphere created in Fritz Lang's film *M*, which of course symbolized life as it was in Germany in the years preceding the rise of the Nazis; life as it was for Lindner who wanted to leave, for mental as well as social reasons, to flee his country in order to achieve his own personal liberation and his own career as a painter in the United States. Of course, he then had to adapt his fantasies, his fears, his frustrations, his most secret desires to a reality that exerted new pressures, new burdens, and new challenges on every moment of his life.

The adaptation was not made without damaging some aspect of Lindner's fantasy world; or it may be said that Lindner was forced to find new sources of inspiration and creativity. Humor allowed him to pretend that painting was only a game of social seduction, a show, a means of preventing others from penetrating the complex, intimate labyrinth of his soul. Lindner proceeded to intensify and develop what had always been latent in his work; the elements of mystery and intimacy then became obvious and loudly stated.

From the moment humor "saved" Lindner, his paintings became charged with a certain unexpected power. Suddenly, his skills, those giant shields which protect intimacy through "Epinal illustrations" began to fill the space and the life of Lindner in a way that gave him, to his astonishment, a certain social responsibility. People started to take his parade seriously. All of this happened a short time before painters, having grown tired of believing that they could express themselves through action painting or repetitive gimmicks, rediscovered the beauty behind the popular images of the times: cinema posters, luminous signs, magazines, the whole gamut of advertising.

Lindner's secret is his ability to transform art into something other than art — into life, poetry, humor, ideas, feelings, taste, fashion, revolution, counter-revolution. In Lindner's opinion, art is not worthwhile unless it has this capacity to become transformed. Consequently, Lindner's work continually displays a duality; on the one hand, it borders on nothingness and death, and on the other, it affirms the supremacy of the individual, his freedom, his disturbing independence.

The genius of a painter lies in his ability to paint within the limitations of his medium and, at the same time, to go beyond those limitations. I would like to try and understand how painting enabled Lindner to pass off his humor, irony and skepticism for what they are not — mere theatrical convention and playbill posters. Duplicity on the part of the painter, since *The Visitor* was done in 1953, is not likely. In this work, harsh laminations and a certain intimacy fill the canvas. The reason Lindner is called a precursor

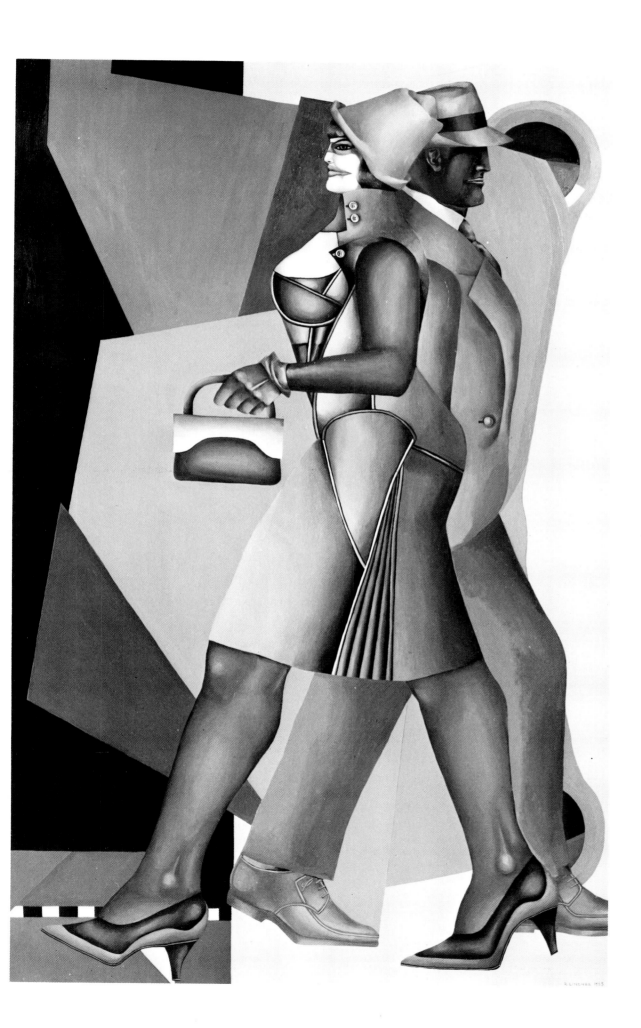

Lollipop. *1968. Watercolor. 61 x 50.5 cm. (Photo Galerie Claude Bernard).*

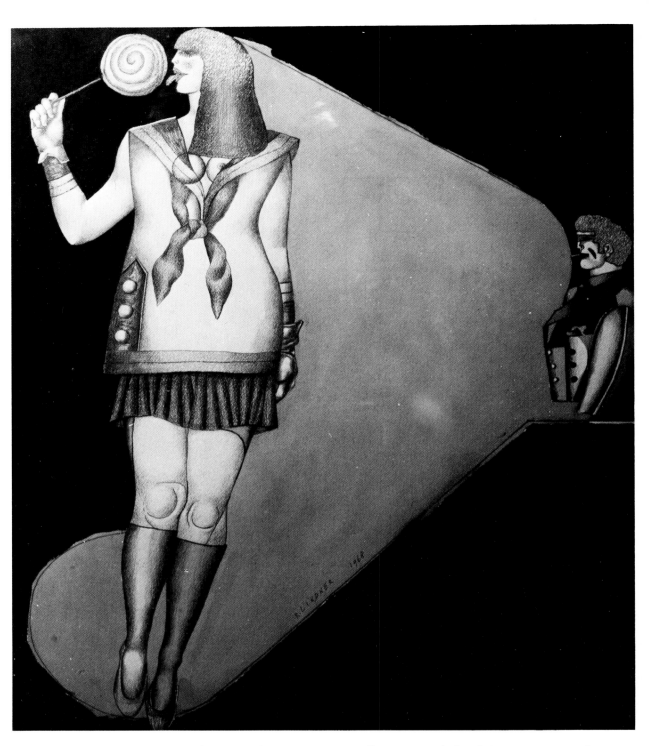

A German emigrant in the United States, Lindner took advantage of the incredible historical misunderstanding in which it is usually possible to recognize not only the special genius of a country but of an entire epoch. Between pre-Nazi Germany and post war New York, Lindner skipped the usual stage — a stepping stone for all the great painters who preceded him and even for some who followed him — Paris. His metamorphosis was easier because he had refused to become captivated or caught up in the society of the Parisian intelligentsia. In New York, he did not have to explain, justify himself, or even define his ideologies. He was free to take on a new face or, as it happened, new masks.

Painting led Lindner to love what had been strangest for him at the beginning, that is American stories of adventure and the world of show business with its Hollywood and Broadway dreammakers. His work is precisely on the fringe of this world, but at the same time, he per-

sonally remained aloof. Upon occasion he seems to identify with a circus rider, an acrobat performing with or without a net, or the Lolita type of prostitute, the adolescent tease. The truth is, Lindner was led by his painting as if he were being pulled by an adventuress in search of challenge and risk. What is surprising, however, is that Lindner dressed up his work, made it sumptuous and brilliant; this then made it inaccessible. But his paintings are not "a superinvestment in intensities just to sell a libidinal labyrinth," as someone once said. They are rather like a huge deck of playing cards which Lindner invented for the great game — his own life. If he seems to have won at this game, so much the better; he might have lost. First of all, he had to think of painting as the highest form of game, a game that could dispel his boredom and sense of separation resulting from exile, a game that might even open a channel for real communication. Lindner might not have been driven to inventing this game at all, if politically and socially on that day in 1933, the world had not shut him out of his own adolescent and romantic dreams.

What is Lindner's "great game" about? The universe created by the act of mating, the simple proximity of a man and woman, the sense of the forbidden, the inviolate space that is formed by their very relationship. Lindner can show, as when he portrays a circus or strip tease performer, the most opaque, subtle and unspoken rapport that exists between two human beings. His capriciousness or humoristic style keeps analysts and other specialists off guard and unable to perceive his depth. Although his works now attract a larger audience, the critics' words still grate and crack; silence is best except for those agitators who insist on speaking out.

The virtue of Lindner's paintings resides in the many implications they convey. The eroticism of the woman, for example, is suggested neither by obscene details nor by her posture but by the sense of waiting that fills the canvas. The women appear to be offering themselves like modern icons, yet their secretive air of restraint and playful dignity make them fascinating. Massive, booted, and crushing like Sacher-Masoch's *Venus in Fur*, they perhaps summon up a fantasy of flagellation but are never caught this way. Lindner endows them with implicit gestures that they are not likely to complete. His aim is to strengthen their emblematic image as "queens of hearts" for a ritual in which one ought to be aware of one's fantasies. As sovereigns over that mental freedom without which real freedom would always be exhausted, they assert themselves as the mistresses of Lindner's great game which does nothing more than give them the space of the canvas and the most solemn and refined attributes to attract recognition. Arro-

103

To Sasha. *1968. Watercolor. 39 x 28 cm. Alexander Schneider collection, New York.*

gant, despotic horsewomen, they nevertheless receive recognition for their place in modern art; they are the anti-Wagnerian versions of the Valkyries, those who gather living men in the street and do not wait to find them as dead heroes on the battlefield before carrying them off to their paradise.

Lindner's ironic lesson: there is no possible happiness other than an artificial one that occurs with luxury; and luxury is in reverie and in acquiring a sense of distance. It is a concept as far removed as possible from banal populism and Pop art. Like Hegel, Lindner shows that the "state of paradise is not perfect" but only an idea of what the perfect state might be like — a myth incarnate. The woman, or more exactly

woman's emblematic image is only the final target of a mental shooting match which for Lindner began even before his painting. His interest in writers which manifested itself from adolescence and continued until his death was partially a result of his desire to keep that distance even vis-a-vis his own painting. Myths cannot be created without this distance which freezes living beings under the glass and protects them from confusion. We can say that Lindner's fascination for women has to do with a choice — his choice. He was not an obsessive person; he imposed obsessions on himself.

Imaginary women, counterparts of real women, are created out of the spontaneous visions of a myth, whether it is *The Eve of the*

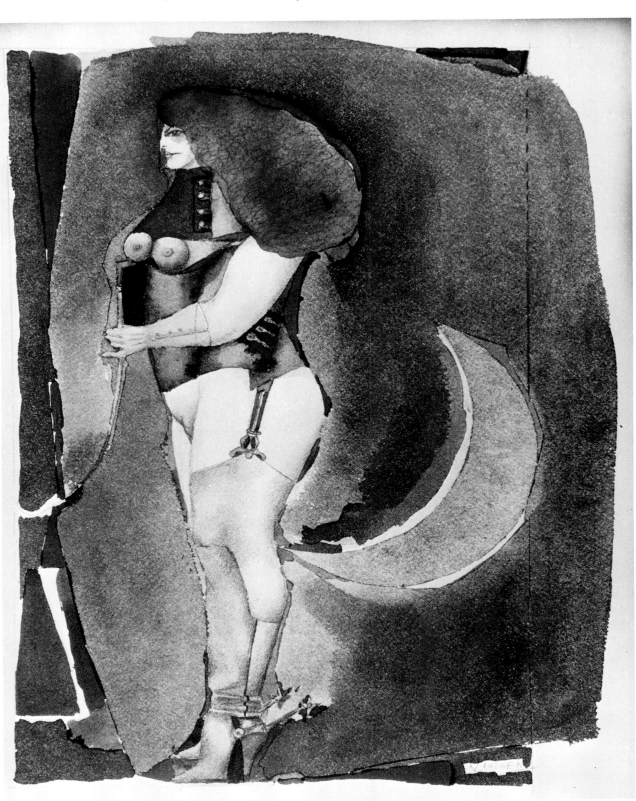

104

Untitled. *1973. Watercolor. 43 x 33 cm. Henri Cartier-Bresson collection, Paris.*

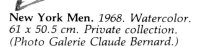

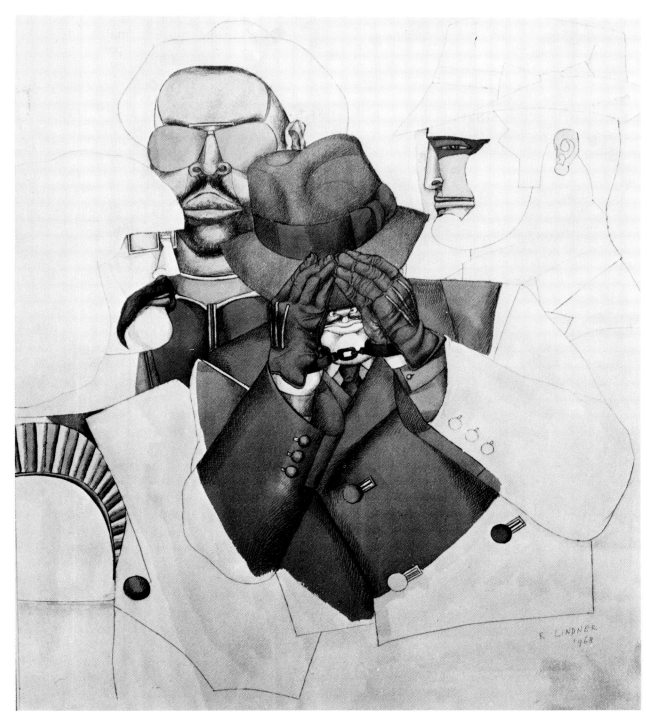

Future of Villiers de l'Isle-Adam or Nabokov's *Lolita.* The relation that we maintain with their images comes from waking dreams that exert a disturbing ambiguity on the images. Only in love are we confronted with troubling characters such as when we recognize in a real woman the image of a buried myth, censured by our resignation to the trials and tribulations of everyday life. Painters, even better than novelists and poets, sometimes know how to impose reality on their exemplary fantasies: from the *Venus* of Titian which served as the model for Manet's *Olympia,* to the sleepwalkers in Paul Delvaux's work, from Ingres' *Odalisque* to *Mémoire* by René Magritte, from *Lucrèce* of Cranach to Victor Brauner's *Chimères,* from the ecstacy of Füseli's *Cauchemar* to the arrogant and all-powerful women of Richard Lindner. Each time a theatricalization of masculine sentiments and desires defines a particular myth — the amorous courtesan, the female victim, the

poet's muse, the female medium, the inaccessible actress, the evil tease, the statue of perfection or the female fantasy machine.

In the history of women as conceived by painters, real women have been assigned a fantasized role. Consequently, from one painter to the next, the symbolic function of the female image changes and the shadow of historical reality intervenes and imposes itself differently between the mythical and the living experience — Delacroix's *Liberté sur les barricades* contradicts the imperial feeling in Ingres' *Odalisque* just as Richard Lindner's women contradict the sense of the tragic in the whores and singers of Toulouse-Lautrec.

Nor is it possible to detach the Ingresque dream of perfection from Napoleonic pomp just as Manet's *Olympia* cannot be separated from the society in which Baudelaire lived with Jeanne Duval and rendered homage to Madame Sabatier. The scandalous nudity of the *Olympia* has the

Arizona Girl. *1975. Oil on canvas. 170 x 198 cm. (Photo Fischer Fine Art Ltd., London.)*

tortions) which depend on the intellectual illusion of theory rather than on classical eloquence. When facing woman, man literally does not know what to think; he forbids himself to dream of her or to accept her as she is. And in analyzing his inhibitions, his mechanisms of repression, woman reminds him of blocks, traumas and taboos. The myth without myth becomes the only myth possible just as painting without painting becomes the only possible painting. But all the while men continue to meet women; they speak to each other; they make love; they quarrel; they leave; they miss each other — life goes on. Painting, like science, has passed in vain through the looking glass (or the "great glass" of *The Bride Stripped Bare By Her Suitors*); yet, we continue to look at ourselves through this glass every morning and every evening from the same perspective.

Since the time of Manet women in paintings have turned their gaze from the one contemplating them, painter or spectator; distracted or distraught, vulgarly made-up or stark naked, sleeping or their backs turned, they ended up surrendering themselves, legs spread apart, to the rape of the sun in rooms created by Balthus. Dreaming of an impossible rape or prostrate with sorrow, they deny the myth of the inaccessible woman — inaccessible because of her perfection as the angel or the madonna — which they have thrown onto the sidewalks and wastelands of Picasso's blue period after having burned it at the café-concert and bordellos of Toulouse-Lautrec. But, scarcely nubile, it is upon entering the dark, semi-deserted apartments, as they look forward to the ecstacy of masturbation that they undertake a different inaccessibility — the island of pleasure that the woman gives to herself. Magritte was the only one who tried to curb the degradation of the myth of the Olympian goddess by transforming his wife Georgette into an ancient statue stained with blood. On this subject, with the exception of Bellmer who explored the physical aspects of woman's erotic sensations, the surrealists — and this is where Xavier Gauthier is right — have desperately tried to do away with the movement which, since *Les Demoiselles de la Seine*, has brought the myth of the woman back down to earth. Breton's cult of Nadja, Dali's of Gala, or Aragon's cult of Elsa have this in common with the cult of a Georgette transformed into *Black Magic* or into *Memory*, that is the rejection of every attempt to vulgarize the beloved and desired woman; the reservations of André Breton with respect to Bellmer become clear from then on. In spite of the factual nature of *Nadja* or *Vases Communicants*, the surrealists refused to bring woman down to earth. The surrealist myths about the female-child and the female-sorceress which Benjamin Péret discussed

air of failure suffered by a poet who had been condemned by the bourgeoisie for his sexual fantasies and who then cultivated its hysteria with "delight and terror." If Baudelaire hesitated throughout his life between two types of beauty — the angel or madonna and the dreadful whore — the pendulum swings in the same way from Ingres to Manet. The history of painting over the last two centuries conclusively proves the need for vengeance which is one of the strongest motives for literary and plastic creation; the need also showed the triumph of moral beauty over the ideal. Even though Gustave Moreau tried to resuscitate the myth of *Salomé*, he provoked the twofold internal contradiction of Rouault and Matisse and myths exploded in all directions. By retaining only the line of the female body, the abstract indication of femininity, Matisse toppled the mythical image of masculine sentiments, feelings and desires in the theater of *distanciation* — the body gave way to an abstract ideal and then to its omission entirely. This progressive *suppression* of the body, the advent of which was perceived by Georges Bataille in the *Olympia*, produced new lies (dis-

Lindner's women speak of sex through clothing
An aggressive female

in his preface to *l'Anthologie de l'amour sublime* all put up real opposition to obscenity, scatology, prostitution, the splendid banality of love-making. In escaping the path of sublimation, Richard Lindner followed Manet, Lautrec and Balthus. Like them he placed the feminine myth back in the rowdy setting of the great metropolis; banality itself is adorned with the prestigious beauty of myth. The woman becomes sovereign and dominates men by the splendor of her infamous vulgarity. She appears all the more worthy against the background of an everyday life that is celebrated in magnificent colors, with bars, telephone booths and hotels that seem like palaces constructed for a new kind of ruler.

Lindner's women have no nature surrounding them. No trees, waterfalls or forest reminds us that it is the female species that bind us to this planet. In an age in which nudity and pornography are in fashion, Lindner has invented women who speak of sex via their clothing and form; thus, Lindner equips and harnesses them as circus riders, Lola Montezes, the Blue Angels of the opera, etc. A strange reversal: the fantasy of a surrendering woman, offered nude to the viewer (almost in the old style of the court painters) as if she were a platter of fruit, has been replaced by a woman who appears to resist, who dominates with whip in hand, a world of lonely clients. Instead of the paternal gaze of a man looking on a submissive, willingly vanquished woman, Lindner offers an aggressive female. His paintings are powerful and fascinating because he has been able to debunk the old myths about women; only a few writers until Nabokov had been able to surpass Lindner in this domain; Sade's characterization of Juliette was the first announcement to the Western world that the myth of man being the all-powerful, noble-minded and supreme judge had come to an end.

The bar and the night club, the sun and the moon are in Lindner's work nothing more than abstract symbols for societies and peoples who have adopted artifice as the rule of daily life. The couples in these settings are like advertisements for a purse, a sweater, a derby, necktie, hair style, models assuming a pose in facing the lens. Nothing binds them to one another except the theatrical and very artifice of their disguise; it is as if they had decided not to reveal what they really are, as if their psychological reality had been effaced for the sake of the *appearance* of mystery and amorous, sexual complicity. The viewer could hardly tell who precisely these characters are in Lindner's paintings: elegant men dressed as pimps and gangsters, bourgeois women pretending to be whores and circus riders, or real gangsters and real whores. Representational theater brings out the

extremes of each social class; these characters, who nevertheless embody an era, still do not correspond to any particular social or historical reality: The New York of the sixties and seventies is superimposed on the Berlin of the twenties, the lumpenproletariat on the aristocracy, debauchery on sophistication, or stalls at a fairground over the solitude of an empty room.

Richard Lindner, the voyeur of the big city, was always on the lookout for what could move him; when he was sitting with his friends or speaking to them in a restaurant, he would cast a furtive glance at neighboring tables. In New York he loved to sit at the Brasserie facing the staircase going down to the basement so that he would not miss the black pimps and their impressive prostitutes dressed in silk dresses and white furs when they went down there at midnight. Everything that pertained to couples passionately interested him. He was interested in

Two. 1976. Oil on canvas. 203 x 153 cm. (Photo Galerie Maeght.)

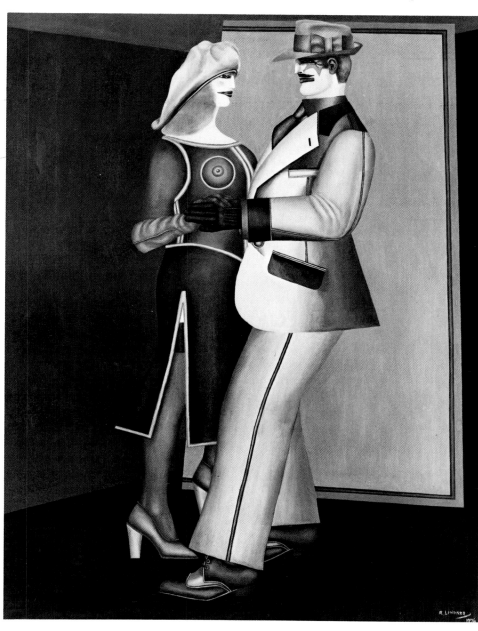

them as much as if not more than he was concerned about the social life of painters, unless it was a question of strong, eccentric personalities like Balthus or (before his death) Max Ernst. Most of the time his conversation turned to the cities themselves: their taxis, elevators, hotels, air-conditioning, telephone systems, restaurants and museums. In his eyes, Berlin, Paris, New York continued to offer the greatest theaters and the grandest forums for the imagination. He distrusted all other cities, as if the world were an arid, boring province that he was compelled to fly over from time to time in order to join one of the cities he loved to another and reawaken in himself their fantasmagoria. In looking at his painting it is clear that he proceeded with colors, with forms as well as people, and in the same preferential system. In this respect his paintings are dressed-up monuments, a *tabula rasa* to eccentricity.

Occasionally, in thinking of Lindner, I'm reminded of the story of Baudelaire who once pretended to give in to a woman that used to sit opposite him every day at the café La Belle Poule. At her insistence, he finally invited her to his house, watched her undress and then rest her lovely fingers on the back of an armchair; he still did not say a word as she placed her bare foot at the end of her hair so that he could admire its length. Then, when Cladel who was accompanying them discretely disappeared, Baudelaire told her to get dressed. Lindner, like Baudelaire, liked beautiful beings and objects too much to let himself in for the slightest disappointment. He avoided closeness, preferring to imagine from a distance with a kind of ironic nostalgia what he knew he could not deal with intimately. His prudence and fears were so excessive that he went to the extreme of protecting himself from his own portrayal of women by wrapping them in imaginary clothing that served both as armor and as masks. The enemy of contagion and promiscuity, he projected their images on a screen from which they could not descend to disturb him. Then, as he finished a painting after one or two months of work, he began to take his distance, like a regular theater goer who leaves before the last act is over because he anticipated the finale. Having spent so much time on a painting glazing layers of color, Lindner's enthusiasm gradually diminished. In fact, he became bored with perfecting his work and wanted a change of subject, a distraction. However, his needs, his preferences and manias were such that he merely changed the scenery and costumes for each painting. Each time, the same actresses and actors reappear with only subtle variations and in very nearly the same roles. In one painting, Lindner changes a wig, in another trousers and shoes; elsewhere a dog sits between the protagonists, but it always involves

the same psychological game, namely the dramatization of life between couples along with the dramatization of appearances in the lives of adventurers and lonely people. The substance of the painting remains its esthetic form, the anarchic liberty of gangsters and philosophical and social forms.

In my recent visit to Berlin, I spent many nights in bars where an astonishing group of night people congregated; the bars were open till dawn. Around three or four in the morning, you could see a transvestite coming in and putting a poodle on the knee of a favorite customer, noisy women with white powder on their faces throwing themselves on their neighbors and talking about Nietzsche, intellectuals with big round glasses drinking champagne and swearing that they prefer suicide to murder, elegantly dressed pimps with taciturn faces, despairing artists, falsely debonair and bloated with beer, and a few other undistinguished types, all eccentrics: a veritable collection of Lindnerian characters in the raw. At the Zwiebelfisch, for example, I felt as if I had wandered by chance into the lives of the characters in his paintings, their silence was broken and a Germanic cosmopolitan from another epoch, from his American paintings, seemed to speak. I recognized there not only what intellectuals call the "return of the repressed " twenties in Germany and the degradation of the ideals of romanticism but also the nocturnal catharsis of people, who having lost their identity with and through Nazism, are desperately seeking to have what remains of their spirit coincide with American ideology. The more I thought about it, as I listened to my neighbor who took me for a New Yorker tell me in English that each person is right in his own way, in his own individuality — the assassin in assassinating, the bourgeois in trying to keep comfortable, the revolutionary in taking risks, the poet in his poetry — the clearer Lindner's paintings became to me. I felt as if I had at last begun to approach his hidden truth. The white faces, the redheads, the animal fur of my Nietzschean interlocutor who had shooed away her companion with a flip of her hand so that she could speak to me more easily all gave her words an air of significance; it was as if I were witnessing a dramatic demonstration of an intimate secret.

Painter of a fantastic double game (European-American, German Jew-Parisian), fleeing Europe for America and America for Europe, it may be that Lindner decided to paint in order to create the parade (of events and characters with their violent component) of all the successive settings during his lifetime: a Nazi-anti-Semitic environment in Germany, competition and frantic individualism in France, gangsterism and money in the United States. The women he pain-

Drawing. 1977-1978.
(Photo Piotr Trawinski.)

110

ted were the shields whom he invented to protect himself from those dangers that he feared could return, like vultures, to his life. He endowed women with guile and wiles, with occupations as dubious actresses and as madams of metaphysical brothels as if he were entrusting them with a personal mission to act as a buffer against powerful social forces. We admire these women as much as we detest them, to some extent because they never really embrace any nation or any political ideology.

For Lindner, men are only playing cards in the lives of women. They must either conform or remain excluded from the female's game. In yielding, however, a man can upon occasion and by chance win. Lindner's paintings in general bear the mark of an apparent submission to rules laid down by others: women, institutions, the large cities or the industrial world. Lindner's achieved freedom, first, by pretending to give it up. But his admiration of the female force was also his way of circumventing the rules. Some women feel a certain malaise in his paintings due possibly to the fact that they see themselves simultaneously celebrated in their new dominant role and held at a distance. Lindner endows the female with the same rainbow of colors that he gives to the male, but he exhibits her in the foreground and in such a unique manner — for example, the heel of her shoe is placed at the height of a man's chin — so that she finds

herself as alone in her sovereignty as she was in her real slavery. However, Lindner does not judge or idealize women; nor does he condemn them. For the first time in the history of painting he gives them the mythical image of dominator of reality without which no society in the world today could advance.

Even if the myth is false and shown to be as dangerous as the myth of the omnipotent man, Christ Pantocrates or Stalin, Leonardo da Vinci or Einstein, the myth of the all-powerful woman can temporarily help to change the implicit rules of civil society: it is the historical function of this new lie. The intellect, the genius of Lindner, resides in his ability to maintain a certain distance or objectivity in painting this myth so that neither man nor woman become its dupes for very long. "We never know the living," said Kafka. But Richard Lindner painted real living beings which is perhaps why his paintings remain unfamiliar and only half understood by them. One day, perhaps in twenty or thirty years, his work will be seen as a prism, silent but irreplaceable, of the change that occurred in the twentieth century in the relations between men and women. Their present lies may serve as a basis for a future truth which is now unknown to both of them and which will certainly be very disconcerting: the infinite femininity of men and the infinite masculinity of women.

ALAIN JOUFFROY

richard lindner: 1901-1978
by john gruen

In an interview ten days before his death, Lindner talked about Weimar Germany, his past and the women who had haunted him. The works in his recent New York show — the first in ten years — are a disturbing and unique testament to his vision.

Richard Lindner was an artist of extraordinary gentleness whose work dealt almost exclusively in cruelty.

His imagery fixed on the bizarre low-life of his native Germany transmuted into sinister American nightmares drenched in garish New York colors. With stiletto precision, he shaped male and female figures of supreme hostility whose encounters produced a ferocious sexuality. No other 20th-century painter has depicted women with greater fanaticism or greater eroticism. A savage lust informs their monumental geography and the promise of their embrace implies instant annihilation.

And yet Lindner saw these rapacious creatures as mythic goddesses, sacred beings consumed by secret desires. Dressed in outrageous garb or seen in terrifying nakedness, they emerge as fantasy figures of unthinkable potency. Their icy grandeur creates a devouring heat, and the men seen within this ambiguous climate seem themselves enthralled by the voyeuristic dramas which Lindner invented with such cool.

During the mid-60's Lindner's paintings were mistakenly swept into the vortex of Pop art. It was assumed that the stark immediacy of his mundane subject matter — pimps, whores, killers, cruel dogs and mad parrots painted in slick, glistening colors — was the product of contemporary experience and the celebration of seamy American life. In point of fact, Lindner predated Pop by nearly 20 years, during which time the artist was considered something of an outsider — someone whose stylistic roots seemed firmly planted in constructivist soil. Indeed, the immaculate geometry of his figures can easily be translated and isolated into abstract structural shapes — circles, squares, triangles, which in turn re-emerge as the components of figurative elements — breasts, eyes, shoulders, legs.

Again, the sensibility that informs his subject matter is not an American Pop sensibility (although America was Lindner's pictorial hunting ground), but one that long had been immersed in European culture and derived its impetus from old-world bourgeois life and standards. Still, the razor-sharp quality of his technique, the almost abrasive glare of his light, and the startling nature of his pictorial content ultimately brought Lindner's pictures within the ambience of Pop art and, much to his surprise, the movement helped to catapult his name into the forefront of American art.

Two days before the artist's death on April 16, 1978, at the age of 76, Richard Lindner agreed to an interview. His first major exhibition in New

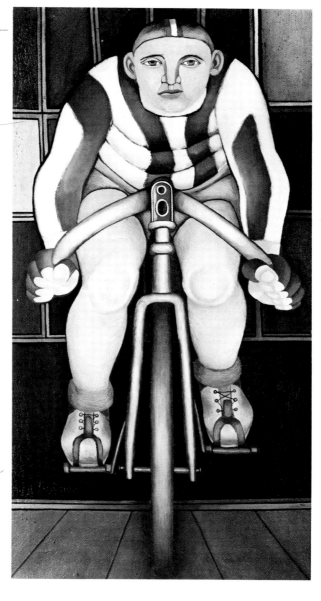

Cyclist. *1951. Oil on canvas. 101.5 x 51 cm. Kunsthalle, Hamburg.*

111

York in ten years had just opened at the Sidney Janis Gallery and Lindner had traveled from his home in Paris to be present at the opening. The exhibition found the artist in dazzling form, with canvas after canvas producing their familiar *frisson* of malevolence. Lindner's creative vigor had not diminished — indeed, had intensified and coalesced into an ever terser and more eloquent statement of pure form and gorgeously poisonous color. And the atmosphere of threat and apprehension that inhabited each work continued to wield its disquieting power.

Lindner looked very frail at his opening. A short, small-boned man with sad, questioning,

112

Boy. 1955. Oil on canvas.
96 x 66 cm. The Nelson
Foundation collection.
(Photo Geoffrey Clements.)

pale blue eyes, he had complained of being unable to shake a recent bout of Russian flu — a bout that caused him to lose some 15 pounds. Still, he seemed delighted to see the many friends and visitors who had come to greet him and to celebrate his opening. With him was his wife, Denise, an extremely pretty French woman 40 years Lindner's junior. During the opening, a date was set for an interview. "We'll have an elegant lunch, and then we'll go back to my apartment and talk," Lindner told me.

The lunch a few days later was indeed elegant and the artist seemed in fine spirits. I learned that his wife had returned to Paris. "She loves New York, but likes Paris better," said Lindner. "Denise is a very good artist, but for some reason, she refuses to show her paintings. It's really very strange."

During lunch Lindner explained that although he had been living in Paris for many years, he had always kept an apartment in New York.

"Paris is so boring! I need to recharge myself by coming back here all the time. Actually, all the sketches for my paintings are made in New York. Just to see the color of a New York truck or taxi excites me! There's life in New York. Paris is dead. All the ideas for my paintings come from what I see here. Then I go back to Paris and paint pictures. I've not shown in New York for ten years because there have been several retrospectives of my work in Europe. Also, I wanted to remove myself from the New York scene. My last show here was with the Cordier & Ekstrom Gallery ... finally, it didn't work out and I left them. I don't know ... I suppose my feelings about New York are unjust. I mean, I've never had a bad review, but somehow I've never really had any real recognition in America. Critics and museum people just never knew what to do with me or where to place me. In Europe my work hangs in the best museums, and things are not so confusing. To tell you the truth, I wouldn't like to be a young painter living today. I wouldn't know how to begin here!"

Lunch over, we strolled a few blocks to Lindner's apartment in the East 70s. Comfortable and immaculate, the modern living room had been turned into a studio. A specially constructed easel, with small pulleys and cranks, stood near the windows. A charcoal sketch of a man with a bowler hat rested upon it. We sat on a wide, low leather couch and Lindner began to recount something of his past.

"Although I was born in Hamburg, my first youth was spent in Nuremberg, the most medieval and the most cruel city in the world. The worst instruments of torture were invented there, like the Iron Maiden. People were thrown into wells. Of course, Hitler made Nuremberg his headquarters. But it was a beautiful city. It

was a city of canals — like Venice. It had rich merchants and it has a great history of art. But even as a boy I was aware of a great coldness there ... something sinister that came out of every crevice of the city.

"My mother was an American. When she was 20 she came to Germany, met my father and married him. They settled in Hamburg. My mother has been dead for many years, but I'm still trying to discover her riddle. Her obsession was to become as European as possible. But she failed. As a child I found her behavior almost grotesque. What I mean is she could never quite reconcile her enormous desire for being a true European mother with her strong puritannical temperament. The harder she tried, the more

113

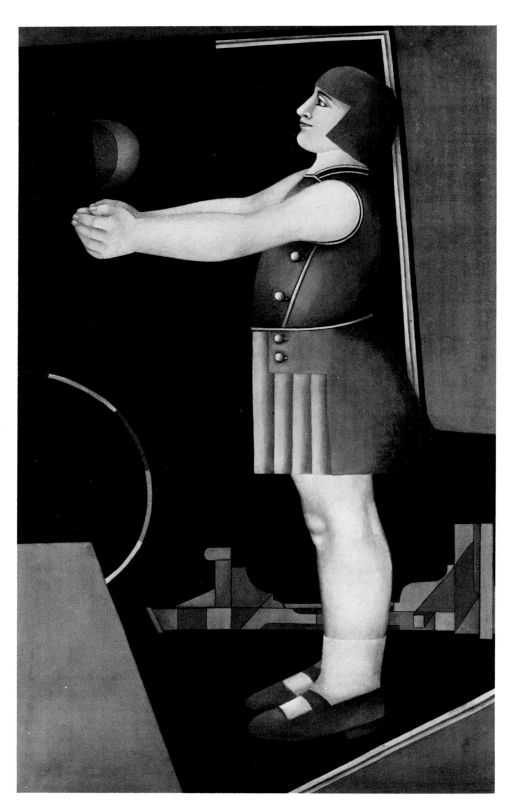

Girl. 1955. Oil on canvas.
127 x 76 cm. Estée Lauder
collection, New York
(Photo Geoffrey Clements.)

bizarre it became. And I became more and more confused as to what she expected of me.

"In a way, she reminds me a little of George Grosz. When Grosz came to America, he wanted to be more American than the Americans. He even wanted to paint like Norman Rockwell! He brought with him an idea of what an American was like. Again, it was a grotesque idea and Grosz failed, just as my mother failed. While Grosz hated the German people he drew and painted, I'm convinced that he was a little like them. You see, one cannot escape what one is."

As a young man, Lindner trained for a career as a concert pianist. During his early 20s he began to concertize and was hailed as a highly promising talent. Becoming a painter had never once entered his mind.

At the age of 24, Lindner moved to Munich. There he met a former school mate who was studying painting at the Munich Academy.

"This friend asked me to visit him at the academy, and when I entered that beautiful old building I was transported. I walked through many hallways and galleries and when I reached his studio I saw two or three artists sitting there painting and smoking and talking. In the center of the room stood a fat naked woman who was posing. The atmosphere was so congenial ... it was like a dream world! Then and there I resolved to stop being a pianist. The fact is, I couldn't stand the pressures of concertizing. I suppose if I had been a real musician I would never have stopped. But I gave up music and applied for entrance at the academy. I was accepted and stayed there for three years. I became a master student. I learned all the basics and my first works were very academic still lifes. I learned how to draw extremely well from very bad painters. I soon found out that from a good painter you never learn anything. Picasso and Matisse were terrible teachers. The only thing a good painter can do is stimulate you.

"Anyway, after my academic training I went to live in Berlin. I lived there for two years — 1927 and 1928. Well, Berlin was a fantastic city. I mean, it was criminal! It was rotten with talent! *Everything* was going on. It was as George Grosz had depicted it, full of decadence and meanness. It was lurid and perverted and marvelous. And so was Paris, when I finally got there. Paris was also rotten, but with big, big talent everywhere.

"I was already married when I got to Berlin, My first wife was a fellow art student at the Munich Academy. We lived together for a few years, and then she fell desperately in love with a writer — a close friend of mine. She didn't exactly leave me, but she lived with the writer. It was an understood relationship — but it took a bad turn. The writer became very ill and died. And after that, my wife committed suicide."

115

Pause. *1958-1961. Oil on canvas. 127 x 89 cm. Mr. and Mrs. Ned Pines collection. (Photo Geoffrey Clements.)*

In 1929 Lindner returned to Munich and took a job as an art director of a well-known publishing firm. When the Nazis rose to power, Lindner escaped to Paris and by 1933 had become active while also continuing to paint. In 1939 the French government interned Lindner for political reasons, but he was released a few months later. At the start of World War II, the artist joined the French army and later the British army. In 1941 he emigrated to the United States and settled in New York, To support himself, he found work as an illustrator for such magazines as *Vogue, Town & Country, Harper's Bazaar* and *Fortune.*

"There wasn't much of an art world in New York when I came here," said Lindner. "There were two or three galleries, and nobody sold anything . I met all the New York artists, but I was always an outsider. I didn't fit in. You see, I wasn't part of any movement. I made a good living as an illustrator, but I got very tired of it. Actually I didn't begin to be a full-time painter until 1950 — there was always something interfering. But then, in 1950, I started to make time for myself. By 1952, I decided to take a teaching job. I taught at Pratt Institute for 12 years. Later I taught at Yale, but that was only for a short time. Actually I didn't like teaching. I taught because I wanted time to paint."

Speaking very softly and with a slight German accent, Lindner discursively began to touch on what lay behind his paintings — the strange scenarios which, he claimed, came straight out of his imagination.

Discovery. *1962. Oil on canvas.*
91.5 x 71 cm. Private collection.

Pillow. *1966. Oil on canvas.*
178 x 152 cm. Zwirner collection,
Germany. (Photo Geoffrey Clements.)

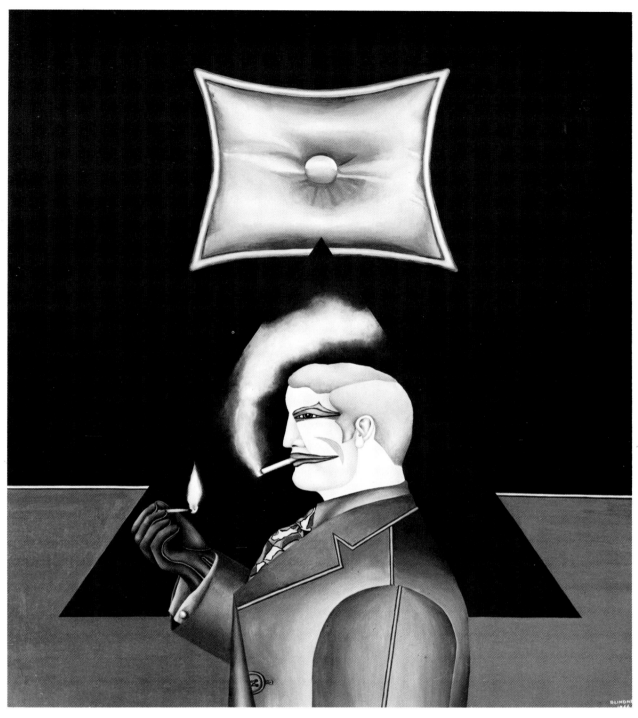

"Subject matter for me is always a man, a woman, a child and a dog. Dogs, like children, are the real grown-ups. And dogs and their owners have always amused me. The other day I was in an elevator and there was an old lady holding a poodle. She said to it, 'Say hello to the nice gentleman!' Germans love German shepherds because they can command them — Germans love to command. Anyway, I never use a model. Models disturb me. They want to talk, and I don't like that. I never do color sketches. I do color on the canvas.

"About color: I have always felt that in order to be a good painter one should be color-blind, because color doesn't have to be seen. It needs only to be felt. When I told that to some of my students, they thought I was crazy!

"Anyway, my paintings have a lot to do with balance and composition. I like structure. As for the women in my paintings, you have only to look at my wife to know that the women I paint are not at all my type. Sometimes the women are very big for reasons of pictorial balance. But, of course, those women have haunted me. Still, I have never really been hurt by a woman. All my women have stayed friends. No. I'm not in the least attracted to the kind of women I paint. However, I think that one must deal with one's complexes ...

"Of course, there is the bordello aspect to my women, and the criminal aspect. Of course, we are all criminals — it's all a matter of degree. Crime is as human as being charitable. Naturally we must have tribal laws. But crime ... crime is

Number 6. *1965. Watercolor, pencil, collage. 49.5 x 39 cm. (Photo Galerie Claude Bernard.)*

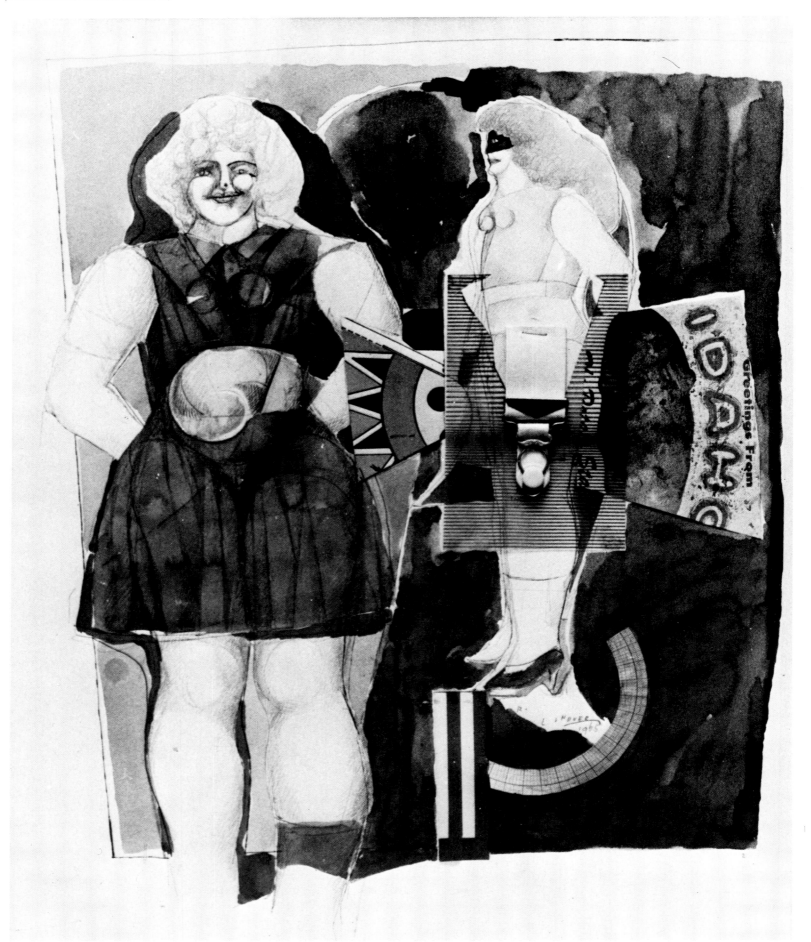

118

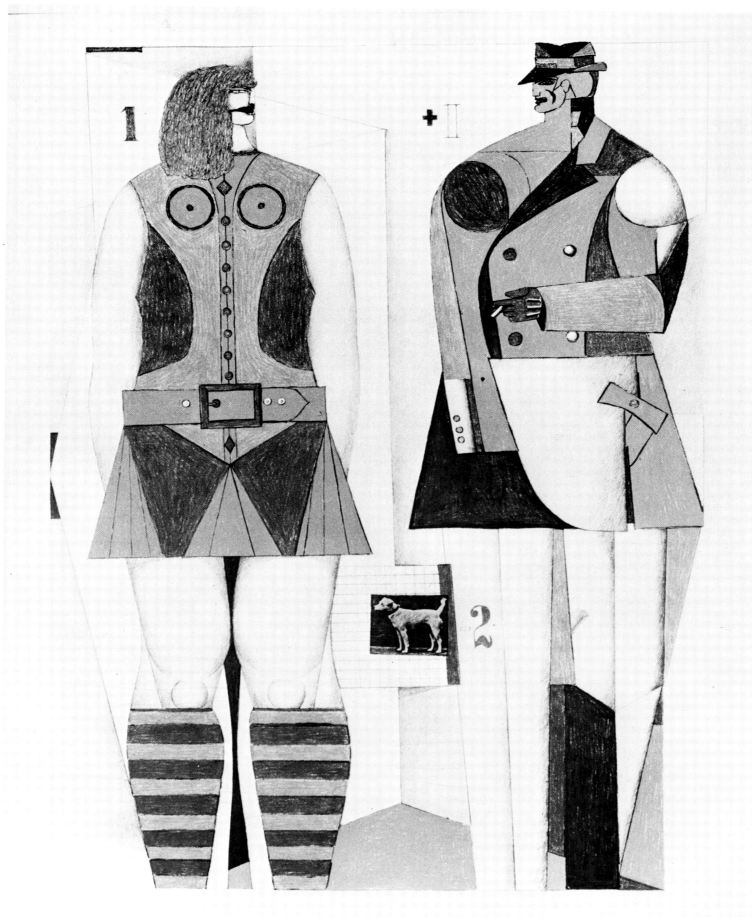

For Adults Only. *1967. Watercolor and pencil. 101.5 x 52.5 cm. Private collection. (Photo Geoffrey Clements.)*

120

like art, and the artist has always understood the criminal. The fear of the criminal is the same as the fear of the artist: both are terrified of exposure. It's basic to their nature.

"But women ...! When I paint them, it's an expression of pure love. I could put this love into any medium. I could put it into sounds. I could put it into words. Actually, I was talking about this to Bill de Kooning. Bill and I are always being accused of being women-haters. The fact is, we love women. I'm looking forward to the day when a woman is president. It's the most logical role for her. With a woman as head of state, there would be no wars. Take her vanity — it all goes into the mirror; it would never affect her role as leader. Man's vanity goads him into all sorts of destructive activity. Luckily women are changing all that.

"Already I sense how men are having a harder and harder time proving their manhood. Women have found out their secret. And men are losing their feathers by the minute. Man's secret is that his so-called manhood is a myth. It's a 19th-century concept that's been fed and nurtured and swallowed by generations of women, who, in the meantime, have had all the time and years to strengthen and deepen their own mystery and power.

"Today women look at men as mystic strangers. Not at all, mind you, as weaklings or creatures devoid of character or substance, but as strangers — mystic beings without any real secrets. Man's touted enjoyment of sex, for example. It no longer worries women. They're enjoying it just as much, if not more, than men. And they enjoy it openly and fearlessly. Man's ego is being changed by all this, and it's beginning to worry him. Women have a greater sense of fantasy. At the same time, they are far more realistic than men.

"And they are wonderfully in command of themselves! Have you ever watched a woman bathe? They do it ever so slowly, almost in slow motion. They observe themselves as though they were works of art. They linger and pause, and they move as in a trance. Beautiful! Beautiful and endlessly fascinating!"

Lindner paused, closed his eyes and savored the thought. In a moment he opened his eyes, smiled and added, "Of course, they *are* terrifying! But, you know, my work is really a reflection of Germany of the 20s. It was the only time the Germans were any good. On the other hand, my creative nourishment comes from New York, and from pictures I see in American magazines or on television. America is really a fantastic place! That's why I admire Andy Warhol so much. He's not a great painter but he's an extraordinary stimulator. He really opened America's eyes to the beauty of the utilitarian,

My work is a reflection of Germany in the 20's

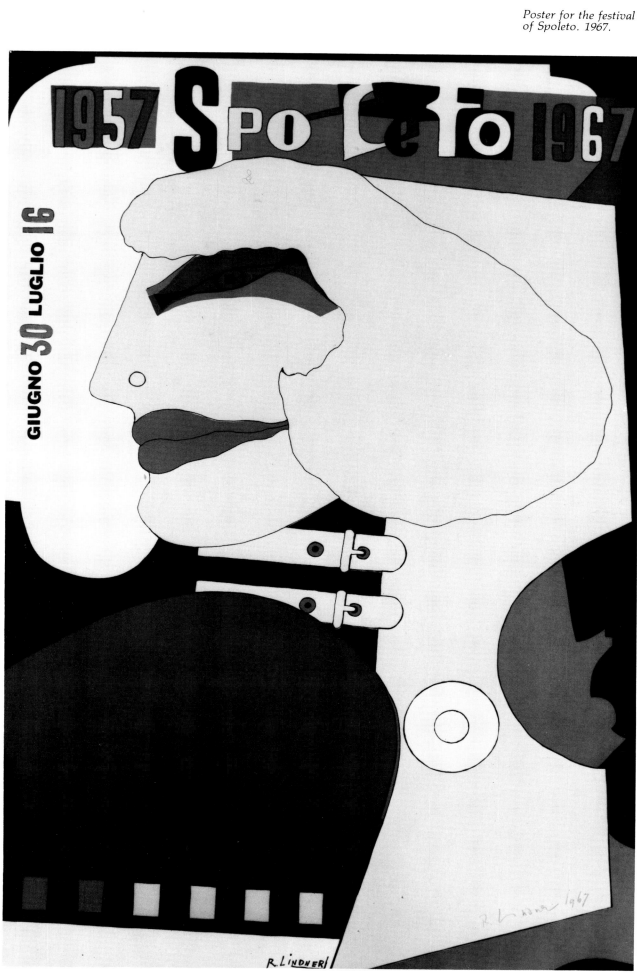

121

A Friend. *1969. Watercolor.*
61 x 50.5 cm. (Photo Galerie
Claude Bernard, Paris.)

everyday object — to the importance of the can!

"I admire the Pop artists — Warhol and Lichtenstein and Oldenburg — but I'm not one of them — never was. My real influences have been Giotto and Piero della Francesca, timeless and ageless artists. I look at them all the time! And I hope that something of their strength has come into my pictures. Basically it's what I'm aiming for — that kind of structural solidity ... that kind of power!"

The interview had come to a close. Two days later, Richard Lindner died in his sleep. The works he created will remain a disturbing and unique testament of an artist's superb craftsmanship, orginality and vision.

JOHN GRUEN

biographical notes on richard lindner

by maïten bouisset

1901

November 11, the birth in Hamburg of Richard Lindner into a middle class family of Jewish extraction. His parents moved to Nuremberg when he was three months old, and it is in this city that he spent his childhood and completed part of his advanced studies.

Of his father Richard Lindner remarked: "He was a nice man; I liked him, but he was a coward. He put everything off on to my mother, which made her a rather imposing person." His mother, an American by birth and "not very intelligent," was a strict puritan. "We were living in the Victorian era," commented the painter who stressed the oppressive and somewhat repressive atmosphere of his home.

One of Lindner's uncles, a popular song writer for variety shows, also must be mentioned. He was undoubtedly the inspiration behind the painter's creation of the male show director who appears in one of his earliest paintings, *The Visitor* (1953). His aunt, "a local beauty," figures in *The Meeting* (1953) beside a young student who bears the features of the artist himself.

Lindner had a younger brother and a sister, a famous opera singer, seven years older than himself. Her premature death at the age of nineteen was certainly one of the most painful and haunting events of his childhood. In one of his watercolors from the fifties, *Sunday Afternoon*, he evokes the feelings of the young boy who, every Sunday in the company of his parents, had to pay a visit to the cemetery.

Apart from family, historians and critics of Lindner's work emphasize the influence of the city in which the painter spent the first twenty years of his life — Nuremberg, "the most medieval and cruel city in the world," "a city founded on secrecy, brutality and mystery," according to Lindner himself, the ancient city of Albrecht Dürer and Hans Sachs, celebrated for the tortures that were practiced there during the Middle Ages, and, from the beginning of the nineteenth century, for its mechanical toy industry. We know that Lindner adored these toys and that he continued to collect them with a strong Baudelairean passion throughout his life. "My references were to toys because I grew up in Nuremberg, the city of toys."

Nuremberg was also the avant-garde center for the theater, the circus and the variety shows, all of which greatly influenced the development of Richard Lindner's future work. Furthermore, it is in Nuremberg that the young artist discovered the plays of Hauptmann, Strindberg, and, above all, Wedekind.

Finally, it is in Nuremberg that Lindner eventually formed a friendship with the writer Hermann Kaestner, and after which, as a general rule, he tended to seek out the company and friendship of more writers than painters.

1922

Raised in a cultivated environment — his father associated with Nuremberg's intellectual elite — Lindner decided very early on an artistic career. "I was born at a time when you could be either an artist or a criminal," he said readily. His family, it should be noted, was not at all opposed to his vocation; to the contrary.

At first, he studied music. His parents had him take lessons with the best musicians in the city. Then he took courses at the Kunstgewerbeschule in Nuremberg where he prepared for a career as a pianist. By the time he was twenty, he was playing in concerts.

1924

He went to Munich with the intention of continuing his studies, also at the Kunstgewerbeschule. Suddenly, following a visit to a painter friend at the Academy of Fine Arts, he decided to end his career as a pianist and study painting. He stayed at the Academy until 1927, and was later to say, "My earliest works were very academic still-lifes." He owned a reproduction of Picasso's *Three Musicians* which shocked his extremely conventional professors, and for a while, he considered going to the Bauhaus.

In the twenties, Richard Lindner followed a traveling circus and made several posters to advertise the show. Then, while a student at the Munich School of Fine Arts, Bertolt Brecht noticed his work and suggested he paint the stage sets for *The Threepenny Opera.*

1927-28

He spent a year in Berlin — "a sinister city, perverted and marvelous."

1929

Richard Lindner returned to Munich, married a student who, like himself, had attended the Academy of Fine Arts, and became the art director of an important publishing house, Knorr and Hir, which published, among others, the works of Thomas Mann.

At the time, Munich was the center of Bavarian culture. Its hero was King Ludwig II who often crops up in Lindner's paintings. In an interview granted to Wolfgang Georg Fischer in July 1973, the painter discussed at length his life in that city during those years preceding the Nazi's rise to power: a provincial city, "especially where art is concerned...there was practically no art in Munich...only a bourgeois type of art" which was discussed at the Cafe Heck. Lindner used to sit at a table there and observe characters from "Simplicissimus", that is, Hitler, Strasser and Goering.

Hitler used to go walking with a dog and held a riding crop in his hand. Dressed in an extravagant manner, he tried to copy the sartorial style of the artists, hoping to be accepted by them. Later on, in 1968, Lindner conjured up this char-

Jacqueline Asleep.
1937. Pencil.

124

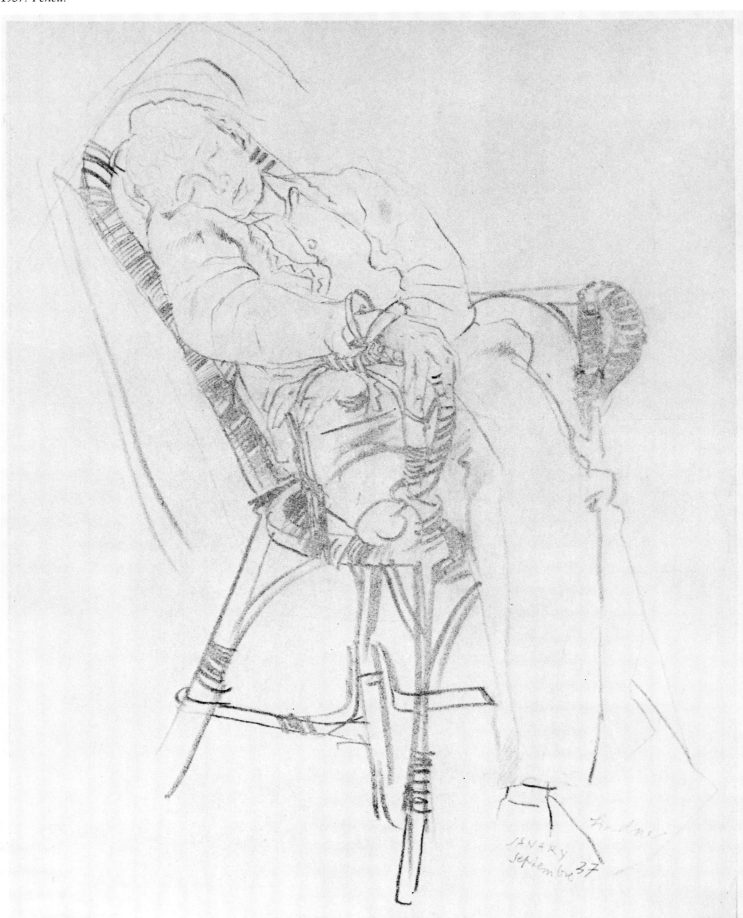

SANARY
Septembre 37

acter in a poster he created for an American theatrical production of *The Resistible Rise of Arturo Ui.*

1933

As a contributor to a socialist political journal, an active member of the Social Democrats and a Jew, Lindner was closely watched by the Nazis. He described how one afternoon in 1933, about the time of the Rohm Putsch, he realized as he was leaving a movie theater that Hitler had come to power and that he would have to leave Germany immediately. Without even taking the time to go home, he left for Paris. One week later, his wife joined him.

Life was difficult for him in Paris. Jacqueline, his wife, worked as a draftsman and designer, while here and there he created a movie poster. Aside from several gouaches in the realistic vein which showed the Parisian landscape as it appeared from the windows of the different dwellings, he painted very little during this period. When people asked him about his pictorial activities during the seven years he spent in Paris, he replied: "Paint? I had too many problems just surviving."

He lived in Montparnasse "like everybody else." Among his acquaintances and friends were Gertrude Stein, Picasso, Andre Gide, Andre Malraux and the Mann brothers. He was also one of the rare artists to maintain good relations with Céline and spent time with the cosmopolitan bohemians of a Paris that little by little saw the descending shadows of the Second World War.

Involved in helping other German refugees, Richard Lindner said on several occasions that exile was cruel and difficult for him.

1939

Throughout France, but especially in Paris, people were beginning to harass the refugees. For Lindner and some of his friends, life seemed a cruel repetition of the Germany of 1933.

Arrested when war was declared for being a German and "consorting with the enemy," he was imprisoned at the Palais des Sports and released five months later. He entered the French army and still later tried, but without success, to join the British Army.

1940

When France fell, he was interned again, at Blois, before being singled out to guide the German troops invading the country. Fully aware of the new dangers before him, Lindner fled on foot across France, reached unoccupied territory and then Marseille. With the help of American relief organizations, he reached Lisbon in March 1941 and sailed for the United States. His wife, also interned, eventually managed to reach New York. A few years later, they got divorced.

Before leaving Europe, Richard Lindner tried to get his father out of the concentration camp. But in vain. Not long afterwards, his father died.

During his confinement in prison, Lindner had sketched an entire series of portraits of those refugees in France who had undergone experiences similar to his. He kept the drawings in his possession until he arrived in New York, when unfortunately they were stolen from him and disappeared forever.

1941

Richard Lindner settled in New York. "I arrived with five dollars in my pocket. It became my city immediately. I felt at home, particularly with the pictures of George Grosz's imaginary universe in my possession." Lindner quickly became a brilliant and much sought-after illustrator of books and magazines and worked for such important periodicals as *Vogue, Fortune, Harper's Bazaar, Seventeen* and *Esquire.*

1945

Around this time the painter became friendly with Saul Steinberg — they were living in the same neighborhood and met on the street — Hedda Stern, a painter who was also Steinberg's wife, and Hedda Hoffer, a very talented photographer, all three having arrived in the United States under similar circumstances. He also frequented the New York artistic milieu, particularly that of the German emigres — Kurt Weil, Wilhelm Reich, Einstein, Marlene Dietrich, and the director of *The Blue Angel,* Josef von Sternberg.

In the forties Richard Lindner became friendly with the painter Fernand Leger, exiled for a while in the United States, as well as with Marcel Duchamp.

1948

He became an American citizen.

1950

At the beginning of the year, Richard Lindner decided to devote himself seriously, even exclusively, to painting.

He spent six months in Europe — "in a way, my farewell to Europe" — and began the creation of his first important painting, the Portrait of Marcel Proust, one of the key canvases of his career. "What fascinated me about Proust was his impudent egotism...the portrait itself turns inward; obviously the subject cared only about himself."

To work out the portrait, Lindner held a virtual inquest among all those who had known the writer. During that half-year he spent in Paris, Lindner also worked on a portrait of Verlaine and of Kant, as well as on sketches for two Academicians, for which he did long, fastidious research, gathering documents and information at the Bibliotheque Nationale.

1952

He accepted a post as professor at the Pratt Institute in Brooklyn where he inaugurated a course called "Creative Expressionism." He stayed there until 1965.

1953

Richard Lindner began a large group portrait, *The Meeting*, which hangs in the Museum of Modern Art in New York. It is the most autobiographical of Lindner's work, summing up the totality of his experiences and defining incidentally his future artistic interests. As Werner Spies put it: "It was the point of departure for his works to come," and added that this painting "reflects Lindner's history and sets it down as if it were being recited by heart."

Assembled in the same scene are Lindner's aunt, who held the painter spellbound in his youth, his sister, who is cast as a young girl in a lewd, teasing pose, Ludwig II, depicted as a mythical figure from his native Bavaria, and his first New York friends, Saul Steinberg, Hedda Stern and Evelyn Hoffer. Lindner himself is represented in the costume of a young student. In an interview with Dean Swanson in March 1969, Lindner said: "Students like this one came to *The Blue Angel*. Generally, they dressed as you see them for the cabaret."

Another subject that excited Lindner in his first years of activity as a full-time painter was the world of childhood. The world of secretive and seductive girls, which he shares with Balthus and which appears in several of his paintings, include *Girl Sitting, Girl, The Visitor*, and the world of stuffed, over-fed, insatiable boys, — *Boy with Machine, The Children Dream, One Afternoon*, — no doubt the cruelest of figures in the Lindnerian universe with their diabolical handling of toys. Girl and boy are reuinted in a second painting, *The Secret*, which is dated 1960 and ends the series.

Still on this subject, it is interesting to observe that in 1972, Gilles Deleuze and Felix Guattari, in their book, *Anti-Oedipe*, inserted a work by the painter right after the title. It was *Boy with Machine*, chosen because it best illustrated the small, yearning machine which operates next to society's technical machinery and leads to "a formidable, non-family type of experience that even psychoanalysts fail to grasp."

1954

Richard Lindner's first one-man show at the Betty Pearsons Gallery in New York was followed by two other shows, in 1956 and 1959. Among others, he exhibited two *Academicians* and *The Juggler*. The critic, R. Rosenblum, speaks of "the sophisticated primitive." Even more interesting is the opinion of painter Robert Indiana: "I saw Lindner as a bridge between European Expressionism and the extreme sophistication of the American social milieu."

For sure, this first show was not a commercial success. But it is also true that from then on, Lindner attracted the attention of other painters. and if, in retrospect, his works seemed to be a wet blanket on the all-powerful New York school, he nevertheless acquired the respect and support of Willem de Kooning, Mark Rothko, and Harold Rosenberg.

1956

He received the William and Norma Copley Foundation Prize and gave a series of courses in drawing at Yale University's School of Art and Architecture.

1960

In the early sixties, apart from several works that seem to evoke memories of the past, Lindner became involved in an extremely personal production, marked primarily by urban settings, New York life, and the very peculiar fauna that inhabit some of its districts.

"I am a New Yorker," Lindner said, "a product of New York... The city is an enormous theatre, twenty-four hours out of twenty-four." He added: "My work is really the reflection of the Germany of the twenties. But on the other hand, it is nourished through living in New York, reading magazines and watching American television. America is truly a fantastic country."

1961

Encouraged by his friend Michael Warren, Richard Lindner exhibited at the gallery Warren ran with Daniel Cordier. Subsequently, after Warren's death, Lindner exhibited regularly, until 1967 with Daniel Cordier and Ekstrom. His exhibition there in 1961 marked the beginning of his success. All of his works were sold. One of his paintings in particular went into the Mesnil collection, and Alfred Barr Jr. became interested in his work.

1963

Curiously, it was at a group exhibition in which he took part, "America 63" at the Museum of Modern Art in New York, that Richard Lindner scored a resounding success. The public mistakenly associated him, as did the art critics, with the Pop movement. Speaking of this exhibition, Lindner said: "I wasn't a Pop artist, but most of the critics thought so because I was known only as a figurative painter...for me, Pop was Warhol and Oldenburg." He added, with a touch of humor, "I have a certain European sophistication that, thank God, the Pop artists don't have." Coming back to this subject much later, in fact it was in an interview with John Gruen just two days before his death, Lindner said again: "I admire the Pop artists, Warhol, Lichtenstein, Oldenburg, but I'm not and never was one of them. My real influences were timeless, ageless artists such as Giotto and Piero della Francesca.

A large group painting, a kind of New York counterpart to *The Meeting*, also dates from 1963 — *The Street* (Kunstsammlung Nordhein-Westfalen, Dusseldorf). Lindner commented: "This is my most beautiful painting." It is a work dedicated to the street, that "city jungle" where prostitutes, pimps, gangsters and all sorts of criminals reign, dressed in their peculiar, bold-colored costumes that make them seem like rigid robots. Little by little, whether alone or coupled, sometimes accompanied by a dog, they became the heros of Lindner's world.

1965

Lindner's first exhibition in Paris at the Galerie Claude Bernard. Otto Hahn described the show: "We feel the influence of Grosz and Baumeister. His originality lies in a certain mechanization of tragedy."

That same year Lindner was invited to become a professor at the Hamburg Academy of Fine Arts.

1966

The painter completed a series of very large paintings: *Telephone*, *Hello*, *No*, *Pillow*, and *Ice*, which were shown, for the most part, at the Cordier and Ekstrom Gallery. Monumental, a veritable machine of seduction, masked, with emphasis on a sexual organ or a breast, "the Lindner Venus" affirms a superiority and triumph over the canvas.

The following year Lindner painted a portrait of Marilyn Monroe, *Marilyn Was Here*. Werner Spies saw it as the American counterpart of the *Portrait of Marcel Proust*. "By the homage that he paid her, Lindner has been the only one to free Marilyn from passivity. He represents her as a poisoned fruit, a new Lulu, both an Eve and a Pandora."

1968

Richard Lindner married Denise, and from then on, divided his time between his New York studio and Paris. A series of very important exhibitions were devoted to him in Europe — at Leverkusen, Hanover, Baden-Baden, West Berlin — and in a number of large American cities.

But, although Denise and Richard Lindner spent summers in Paris to escape New York's stifling heat, the painter always prepared and developed his work in the United States. "Paris is an impressionist sort of city," Lindner said. Even if he happened to finish a painting there, the real, deep motivation came from the great American metropolis. In New York, in particular, Lindner accumulated an enormous iconographic documentation, beginning with his daily reading of newspapers, magazines and journals of all kinds. In these, he found an echo of his concerns and a source of inspiration for his pictorial language.

1969

He began a series of twenty-five watercolors, *Fun City*, a sort of panorama encompassing the sardonic folklore of New York life. These have become some of the most authentic chronicles of New York by night.

The first broad monograph devoted to Lindner by Dore Ashton was published by Harry N. Abrams in New York. A little later, the same publisher produced the work of Rolf-Gunther Dienst.

Two paintings, titled *The Couple* and *Two*, were also done that year. Although it was not the first time that Lindner took up this theme (one version goes back to 1961) it was, nevertheless, during the last ten years of his life that he depicted man and woman side by side, yet completely isolated one from the other, their eyes never meeting, in a large number of paintings: *And Eve* (1970, Musée Nationale d'Art Moderne, Paris), *Two* (1969), *Rencontre* (1976), *Couple* again (1977).

1974

The National Museum of Modern Art in Paris organized a big exhibition of all of Lindner's work. The exhibition was mounted thereafter in the museums of Rotterdam, Zurich and Dusseldorf, and the following year, at the Kunsthalle of Nuremberg, the city where Lindner spent the first twenty years of his life and to which he returned for the first time since his departure.

1975

Hilton Kramer's book on Lindner was published by Paul Bianchini Book and the New York Graphic Society, Boston.

1977

A very important retrospective of Richard Lindner's work was organized at the Museum of Contemporary Art in Chicago, while his more recent paintings were shown at the Galerie Maeght in Paris.

1978

New York's Sydney Janis Gallery exhibited the paintings that had been shown in Paris the previous year. Lindner died April 4, a little while after the opening of the exhibition. William Rubin had just proposed organizing a large retrospective of his work at the Museum of Modern Art in New York.

On his easel, he left an incomplete, untitled painting, which was then shown the following year at the Maeght Foundation. This great work, rigorously finished from the point of view of form and perfectly worked out as far as composition, — the tracing further emphasizes this impression — could be considered a dress pattern: "I am like a tailor," Richard Lindner once said. To come to life, the painting needed only the violent, saturated contrasts of color which attract the eye and compel one to notice the painter's obsessions.

MAÏTEN BOUISSET

127